THE ART AND HISTORY OF PERSONAL COMBAT

by Arthur Wise

ARMA PRESS
New York Graphic Society Ltd.
Greenwich, Connecticut

SBN 8212–0445–9

Library of Congress Catalog Card Number 70–179957

First published in Great Britain in 1971 by
Hugh Evelyn Limited at 9 Fitzroy Square, London

First published in the United States of America in 1972 by
New York Graphic Society Ltd.,
Greenwich, Connecticut

Printed in Great Britain by
Jarrold & Sons Limited, Norwich

Designed by Lawrence Edwards

CONTENTS

For Madge and Hubert Westerman

PREFACE

Violence has been an inescapable fact of human life since the beginning of time. It has been the ultimate arbiter of all conflicts between individuals and between nations. In a very real sense, the history of violence is the history of humanity. Man is a violent animal with a veneer of civilised behaviour just covering the surface. It is not surprising, then, that through the years he has given a great deal of thought to the most efficient ways of inflicting physical damage on his kind.

This book is an attempt to trace the development of one aspect of that thought, and the practice that has arisen from it – the aspect of personal combat. It is not directly concerned with mass warfare, motivated by national policy, but with this question: when two men met for the purpose of inflicting physical damage on one another, how did they go about it?

Yet this is to over-simplify. The formal duel of the seventeenth and eighteenth centuries, with sword or pistol, clearly falls within our terms of reference. It was highly personal, in the sense that only two individuals were involved at the centre of it. In the majority of cases the individuals were not strangers to one another; they had a strongly emotional relationship with one another. Again, they were not participating in some game that stopped short of the logical outcome. They were motivated by a determination to do one another to death. But what of other combatants? What of the man with rifle and bayonet advancing up the slopes of Thiepval ridge during the battle of the Somme? He is one man amongst many millions of others, yet when he meets and fights a single member of the enemy, armed like himself, then he is engaged in personal combat, despite the mass combat that is taking place around him. So is the commando or the war-time agent when he stalks his opponent, comes personally to grips with him and kills him. There is, as it were, a relationship between them, not necessarily of hatred but certainly of violence. And this relationship is an essential feature of personal combat.

For this reason the fighter pilot comes within our terms of reference, whilst the bomber pilot does not. In essence, the fighter pilot is concerned with one opponent at a time. He selects a particular opponent and this selection establishes a relationship between them. When he presses the firing button, he does so with the intention of killing a particular individual in an opposing fighter aircraft. His opponent, by being there at all, has as it were thrown out a challenge which he has accepted. Conversely, the activities of the bomber pilot are impersonal. In the first place his target is too far away from him for any personal relationship with it to exist. In the second place when he releases his bomb-load he is not directing it at a particular individual, but at a general target on the ground. In most cases the target is not even human. It might be a marshalling yard or an arms factory. People are killed as a result of his activity, but their deaths are generally incidental to his main intention. Perhaps more important, from our point of view, once the bombs are released there is nothing that the people on the ground can do to prevent them striking the earth and exploding. There is no personal skill they can bring to bear that can influence the event. By contrast, consider the position of two fighter pilots involved in combat with one another. Neither aircraft is markedly superior or inferior to the other. Each has its merits and disadvantages. The dice are not hopelessly loaded against either of the combatants when the combat starts. They start on a basis of reasonable equality, and they pit their individual fighting skills against one another. Both these factors – reasonable equality of opportunity and individual fighting skill – are essential features of personal combat.

It is unfortunate that the current attitude to human violence is to condemn it as 'bestial' and dismiss it. It is an attitude that has much in common with the Victorian attitude to sex. The condemnation is understandable, but the peremptory dismissal means that we refuse to come to grips with the phenomenon and so try to make sense of it. Certainly the use of the word 'bestial' shows how little we know of human violence, since there is not much 'of the beast' about it. Animals,

according to Desmond Morris,* do not engage in the duel as we understand it. According to Morris, animals fight for two reasons – to establish dominance in a social hierarchy, and to establish territorial rights. The human animal fights for both these reasons. Yet much human combat seems to have been concerned with neither of them. The victor of a duel, for example, does not necessarily enhance his social position. Indeed, society has always frowned on his activities, frequently imprisoned him for them and at times gone so far as to put him to death for them. Yet there is a kind of subterranean social approval of male aggression which presents us with an alarming dichotomy. The popular image of the man successful with women, for example, as projected through fiction and through advertising, is of a fighting man, of a physically aggressive creature, certainly not of an intellectual giant. Fighting prowess is very much tied up with the image of sexual success. What the victor of a duel was really concerned with enhancing was not his 'dominance in a social hierarchy' but his self-esteem.

Besides this difference in motivation, the fight itself is different in man from that in other animals. An animal, says Morris, prefers to avoid combat if possible. It would have been unthinkable for the seventeenth-century French duellist to have avoided combat, once the scene for it had been set. Indeed, he positively sought it, even where no good reasons for it existed. The 'threat-signals' in animals – the puffing up of specialised parts of the body and 'aggressive hair-erection' – are designed to dissuade an opponent from engaging in actual combat. Similar signals, of course, are an integral part of human combat, though their intention is frequently different. In the human duel, for example, such signals are not intended to persuade an opponent to avoid combat, but rather to sap his confidence and so diminish his skill in the forthcoming fight. 'As soon as the enemy has been sufficiently subdued, it ceases to be a threat and is ignored', says Morris, of the fight in the animal world. Yet this, in human personal com-

* *The Naked Ape* by Desmond Morris. Jonathan Cape, 1967.

An attack by mounted men on an unarmed crowd. The weapons used are particularly devastating variants of the falchion and appear exceptionally blade-heavy. Such weapons would deal crippling cuts. It is interesting to note that both these weapons are being used exclusively for cutting. The horseman in the centre of the illustration has adopted the classic position of the mounted man using a cutting weapon, by riding alongside his victim so as to cut down with the full force of his arm directly on to head or shoulder. *The Four Horsemen of the Apocalypse.* From the thirteenth-century manuscript in the Bodleian Library, Oxford.

Tilting at the quintain. This was a widely used training method for work with the lance and was practised both on foot and on horseback. The quintain consisted of an upright post with a crossbar mounted on a swivel. A target was placed at one end of the crossbar and a weight hung from the other end. When the target was struck the bar swivelled and the attacker had to take appropriate action in order to avoid being struck on the back by the flying weight. From the fourteenth-century manuscript in the Bodleian Library, Oxford.

Tilting on horseback. The horsemen attack one another on either side of the long tilt-fence. Their wooden lances, couched under their right arms, cross the necks of their respective horses and engage one another across the top of the fence. The fence in this particular illustration is rather higher than usual and the horseman in the foreground has struck his opponent on the front of the helm. The opponent's head appears to be already moving backwards. We should remember that at the moment of impact the closing speed of the two knights approaches forty miles per hour, a speed which, in this case, is sufficient to shatter a lance. The most likely outcome of this particular engagement would be the unseating of the knight who has been struck and the possible breaking of his neck. Other knights can be seen at either end of the fence awaiting their turn to tilt. From the Westminster Tournament Roll in the possession of the College of Arms, London.

r remaint · i · tout ceru qui delfentable loit
e viengne en babilone par force ꝫ par deltroit
a tant ne venra lamiraut nes groit
que il nes honneurt ainſi g fere doit
i folle ſont parfont ꝫ li terrail ſont droit

bat, is the very moment to strike, to deliver the *coup de grâce*. Again, the 'submissive display' is the technique of the animal for acknowledging defeat. It frequently takes the form of running away. A similar display in human combat, however physiologically and psychologically reasonable it may be, is universally condemned as 'cowardice'. Such a reasonable submissive display in battle – 'cowardice in the face of the enemy' – has until very recently been punishable by death. In some societies it still is.

There is, however, one area of human personal combat that has something in common with animal-fighting. 'It is extremely rare', says Morris of animal-fighting, 'for one contestant to kill the other. Species that have evolved special killing techniques for dealing with their prey seldom employ these when fighting their own kind. . . . Prey-attacking behaviour and rival-attacking activities . . . are quite distinct in both motivation and performance.' We might say the same of the professional gladiator in the seventeenth and eighteenth centuries. Men like James Figg and Donald McBane fought in public with sharp swords and inflicted severe wounds on their opponents, wounds from which occasionally they died. McBane admitted to having a special thrust which he considered to be a certain killer in serious combat. Such a stroke he appears to have withheld in gladiatorial combat, because it was his intention simply to incapacitate his man, not to kill him. This kind of fighting might, by a stretch of the imagination, come under the animal category of combat designed 'to establish dominance in a social hierarchy' – the social hierarchy of the professional gladiator. None the less we must regard it as a form of personal combat. Even though its immediate intention was not to kill, it contained all the features of personal combat as we have defined it. There was a particular and personal relationship between the combatants; there was close physical proximity between them; reasonable equality existed between them and success or defeat was dependent on individual fighting skill. Bare-knuckle fighting, clog-fighting,

single-stick play and the *Schläger* fighting of the German universities all fall into the same category.

Inevitably this book is heavily weighted in the direction of the sword, as opposed to other weapons. Equally inevitably, more attention is given to combat and combat theories of the sixteenth, seventeenth and eighteenth centuries than to other periods. This is not really surprising. In the first place the sword has always been the weapon *par excellence* of personal combat. More men have gone to their deaths in personal combat with the sword than with all other weapons put together. In consequence, more human thought and energy has been devoted to the use of the sword than to any other weapon. Almost all theories of personal combat arise out of theories first evolved in connection with sword-play. Again, the period spanning the 'golden age' of sword-play – if one might call it that – is that covering the sixteenth to the eighteenth centuries. Before that, sword-play had been a crude, unscientific affair, and by the end of the eighteenth century it had become so formalised, so hemmed-in by restrictive theory, as to be little different from modern fencing, either in appearance or in intention.

But because the core of the book is concerned with combat with the sword, we should not be misled into thinking that the theories connected with its use are so much history, with no application to our own time. Ideas put forward in the sixteenth century in connection with two-handed sword-play are still in use in modern bayonet-fighting. Principles conceived by Elizabethan fighting men in connection with dagger-fighting are still adhered to in modern combat with the knife.

Finally, it might be said that although this book is concerned specifically with the development and practice of personal combat, it is incidentally concerned with something else, and perhaps with something more important. It is concerned with an area of social history that has been disastrously neglected. Disastrously, because the motivating force behind much personal combat – individual aggression, individual violence – is still with us. Unless we pull it into the open, unless we study it, unless we try to understand what it is that has made men devote so much time to perfecting themselves as fighting animals, how can we ever come to terms with this important aspect of ourselves?

York   A.W.
July 1971

Chapter One

IN THE BEGINNING: EARLY ATTITUDES

Understandably, the early years of personal combat are not well documented. Not until the European Renaissance, it seems, was a man able to wield both a sword and a pen – men like Lebkommer, Sainct Didier and Marozzo. Nevertheless, we have some evidence of the weapons used by earlier men and there is visual evidence in art. There is, too, the evidence of historians, raconteurs and poets who witnessed the exploits of violent men. And there is another technique we can employ; we can build replicas of early weapons. If we have had any experience in the handling of weapons in general, then these replicas will give us some additional insight into the nature of the originals, and the way in which they might have been used.

The story of Cain and Abel highlights at least some of the recognised features of personal violence. These features are relevant to personal combat, though Cain's attack on his brother can hardly in itself be regarded as combat:

'And in process of time it came to pass, that Cain brought of the fruit of the ground an offering unto the Lord.

'And Abel, he also brought of the firstlings of his flock and of the fat thereof. And the Lord had respect unto Abel and to his offering:

'But unto Cain and to his offering he had not respect. And Cain was very wroth, and his countenance fell.

'And the Lord said unto Cain, Why art thou wroth? and why is thy countenance fallen?

'If thou doest well, shalt thou not be accepted? and if thou doest not well, sin coucheth at the door: and unto thee shall be his desire, and thou shalt rule over him.

'And Cain told Abel his brother. And it came to pass, when they were in the field, that Cain rose up against Abel his brother, and slew him.

'And the Lord said unto Cain, Where is Abel thy brother? And he said, I know not: am I my brother's keeper?

'And he said, What hast thou done? the voice

11

Cain Slew his brother Abel. Gen 4ᵗʰ v. 8

of thy brother's blood crieth unto me from the ground.

'And now cursed art thou from the ground, which hath opened her mouth to receive thy brother's blood from thy hand;

'When thou tillest the ground, it shall not henceforth yield unto thee her strength; a fugitive and a wanderer shalt thou be in the earth.

'And Cain said unto the Lord, My punishment is greater than I can bear.'*

The story reveals an attitude which sees personal violence as a challenge to the natural order of things. It is a challenge, too, to authority – in this case, the authority of God. It is not so much that Cain has inflicted death on his brother, since death would have come to Abel inevitably, in the natural course of time. It is that he has overstepped the terms of his office as a human being. The gift of life and death is not in the hands of man, but in the hands of a higher authority. Despite the fact that man has it in his power to inflict death on another, it is a power he exercises at his peril. The fact that Cain appears to be motivated by the very human feelings of bitter disappointment and jealousy in no way diminishes his crime or his punishment. He has killed without the sanction of a higher authority, and he must suffer the severest punishment for it.

This attitude of authority to individual violence is one which has accompanied personal combat throughout human history:

'They that have power to hurt and will do
                                      none . . .
They rightly do inherit heaven's graces.'

But there is another attitude, apparent in the David and Goliath story:

'And there went out a champion out of the camp of the Philistines, named Goliath, of Gath, whose height was six cubits and a span.

'And he had an helmet of brass upon his head, and he was clad with a coat of mail; and the

* Genesis 4, English Revised Version. Cambridge, 1934.

weight of the coat was five thousand shekels of brass.

'And he had greaves of brass upon his legs, and a javelin of brass between his shoulders.

'And the staff of his spear was like a weaver's beam; and his spear's head *weighed* six hundred shekels of iron: and his shield-bearer went before him.

'And he stood and cried unto the armies of Israel, and said unto them, Why are ye come out to set your battle in array? am not I a Philistine, and ye servants to Saul? choose you a man for you, and let him come down to me.

'If he be able to fight with me, and kill me, then will we be your servants: but if I prevail against him, and kill him, then shall ye be our servants, and serve us.

'And the Philistine said, I defy the armies of Israel this day; give me a man, that we may fight together. . . .

'And David said, The Lord that delivered me out of the paw of the lion, and out of the paw of the bear, he will deliver me out of the hand of this Philistine. And Saul said unto David, Go, and the Lord shall be with thee. . . .

'And the Philistine said to David, Come to me, and I will give thy flesh unto the fowls of the air, and to the beasts of the field.

'Then said David to the Philistine, Thou comest to me with a sword, and with a spear, and with a javelin: but I come to thee in the name of the Lord of hosts, the God of the armies of Israel, which thou hast defied. . . .

'And it came to pass, when the Philistine arose, and came and drew nigh to meet David, that David hastened, and ran toward the army to meet the Philistine.

'And David put his hand in his bag, and took thence a stone, and slang it, and smote the Philistine in his forehead; and the stone sank into his forehead, and he fell upon his face to the earth.

'So David prevailed over the Philistine with a sling and with a stone, and smote the Philistine, and slew him; but there was no sword in the hand of David.

'Then David ran, and stood over the Philistine, and took his sword, and drew it out of the sheath thereof, and slew him, and cut off his head therewith.'*

The attitude behind the story is clearly one of approval. The slaying of Goliath by the young David is an example of how a young man, motivated by the highest ideals and beliefs, was expected to behave in such circumstances. Yet the result of the contest is the same as the attack by Cain on Abel. Goliath lies dead, just as Abel did. The approval in one case and condemnation in the other, lies not in the result but in the circumstances. David is not killing on his own behalf. He is an instrument of authority. He kills with the permission of Saul and with the support of the God of Israel. Cain's action is an assertion of his own individuality; as such it is inadmissible. David's action is on behalf of his king and his society; as such it is not only admissible but praiseworthy. These two attitudes to personal violence have been with us whenever one man has met another, bent on doing him physical injury. It seems that where combat is engaged in to further *personal* ends, it is socially deplored. Conversely, where it takes place under some *impersonal* banner – God, or the State – it can be admissible. The modern concept of push-button warfare is the logical outcome of these attitudes.

Goliath, as we have seen, was equipped 'with a sword, and with a spear, and with a javelin', and these are weapons typical of a long historical period. The Assyrians and Babylonians, the Egyptians, Greeks and Romans were all similarly equipped. Preceding them, archaeological evidence shows the existence of similar pointed weapons with blades of flint and other stones. A spear could be produced by lashing a stone to the end of a wooden staff. A knife could be made by binding one end of a long stone with leather, and chipping the other end into some semblance of a blade. Both were suitable for hunting, and no doubt both were used for combat. Bone and horn

* I Samuel 17, English Revised Version. Cambridge, 1934.

were as effective as chipped stone for producing a weapon capable of penetrating flesh. Knives, spears and arrows could be produced from them. Even earlier must have been the discovery that sharpened wood, hardened by fire, could effectively be used as a weapon.

From such weapons arises the idea of penetration of the body of an enemy, as a means of destroying him. But even earlier must have been the discovery of the susceptibility of a body to heavy blows, the idea not of penetration with a point but of crushing or cutting – an idea that produced the club and the first crude axes. Both these ideas – of penetration and crushing – run side by side through the history of personal combat.

And there is a third idea, that of defence. Goliath had his shield-bearer 'that went before him', and 'he had an helmet of brass upon his head, and he was clad with a coat of mail . . . and he had greaves of brass upon his legs'. The purpose of all this defensive equipment was to place it between his otherwise defenceless body and his opponent's weapon. By contrast, David carried no defensive equipment. His only technique of defence was to make sure that no blow fell on him, by getting out of the way of it. He would defend himself when necessary by avoiding his opponent's weapon. So we see in the dawn of history the two principles of personal combat – each subdivided – already established: the principle of attack, either by stabbing or crushing, and the principle of defence, either by interposing some object between the attacker's weapon and one's own body or by dodging the attacker's weapon.

These principles are apparent in the murderous activities of Achilles before Troy. His fighting technique relied on great speed of movement, uncontrolled aggression and tremendous physical strength. The same qualities are present – together with the principles of attack and defence – in his fight with Hector:

'With this Achilles poised and hurled his long-shadowed spear. But illus-

Roberts sculp.

David cutting of the head of Goliath, the Champion of the Philistines.

1 Achilles slaying Penthesilea the Queen of the Amazons. From a vase of 540–530 BC in the British Museum.

2 The fight between Achilles and Hector. From a vase illustration of about 490 BC in the British Museum.

1

2

trious Hector was looking out and managed to avoid it. He crouched, with his eye on the weapon; and it flew over his head and stuck in the ground. But Pallas Athene snatched it up and brought it back to Achilles.

'Hector the great captain, who had not seen this move, called across to the peerless son of Peleus: "A miss for the god-like Achilles! It seems that Zeus gave you the wrong date for my death! You were too cocksure. But then you're so glib, so clever with your tongue – trying to frighten me and drain me of my strength. Nevertheless, you will not make me run, or catch me in the back with your spear. Drive it through my breast as I charge – if you get the chance. But first you will have to dodge this one of mine. And Heaven grant that all its bronze may be buried in your flesh! This war would be an easier business for the Trojans, if you, their greatest scourge, were dead.''

'With that he swung up his long-shadowed spear and cast. And sure enough he hit the centre of Achilles' shield, but his spear rebounded from it. Hector was angry at having made so fine a throw for nothing, and he stood there discomfited, for he had no second lance. He shouted aloud to Deiphobus of the white shield, asking him for a long spear. But Deiphobus was nowhere near him; and Hector, realising what had happened, cried: ''Alas! So the gods did beckon me to my death! I thought the good Deiphobus was at my side; but he is in the town, and Athene has fooled me. Death is no longer far away; he is staring me in the face and there is no escaping him. Zeus and his Archer Son must long have been resolved on this, for all their goodwill and the help they gave me. So now I meet my doom. Let me at least sell my life dearly and have a not inglorious end, after some feat of arms that shall come to the ears of generations still unborn.''

'Hanging down at his side, Hector had a sharp, long and weighty sword. He drew this now, braced himself, and swooped like a high-flying eagle that drops to earth through the black clouds to pounce on a tender lamb or a crouching hare. Thus Hector charged, brandishing his sharp sword. Achilles sprang to meet him, inflamed with savage passion. He kept his front covered with his decorated shield; his glittering helmet with its four plates swayed as he moved his head and made the splendid golden plumes that Hephaestus had lavished on the crest dance round the top; and bright as the loveliest jewel in the sky, the Evening Star when he comes out at nightfall with the rest, the sharp point scintillated on the spear he balanced in his right hand, intent on killing Hector, and searching him for the likeliest place

to reach his flesh.

'Achilles saw that Hector's body was completely covered by the fine bronze armour he had taken from the great Patroclus when he killed him, except for an opening at the gullet where the collar bones lead over from the shoulders to the neck, the easiest place to kill a man. As Hector charged him, Prince Achilles drove at this spot with his lance; and the point went right through the tender flesh of Hector's neck, though the heavy bronze head did not cut his windpipe, and left him able to address his conqueror. Hector came down in the dust and the great Achilles triumphed over him. ''Hector,'' he said, ''no doubt you fancied as you stripped Patroclus that you would be safe. You never thought of me: I was too far away. You were a fool. Down by the hollow ships there was a man far better than Patroclus in reserve, the man who has brought you low. So now the dogs and birds of prey are going to maul and mangle you, while we Achaeans hold Patroclus' funeral.''

'''I beseech you,'' said Hector of the glittering helmet in a failing voice, ''by your knees, by your own life and by your parents, not to throw my body to the dogs at the Achaean ships, but to take a ransom for me. My father and my lady mother will pay you bronze and gold in plenty. Give up my body to be taken home, so that the Trojans and their wives may honour me in death with the ritual of fire.''

'The swift Achilles scowled at him. ''You cur,'' he said, ''don't talk to me of knees or name my parents in your prayers. I only wish that I could summon up the appetite to carve and eat you raw myself, for what you have done to me. But this at least is certain, that nobody is going to keep the dogs from you, not even if the Trojans bring here and weigh out a ransom ten or twenty times your worth, and promise more besides; not if Dardanian Priam tells them to pay your weight in gold – not even so shall your lady mother lay you on a bier to mourn the son she bore, but the dogs and birds of prey shall eat you up.''

'Hector of the flashing helmet spoke to him

once more at the point of death. "How well I know you and can read your mind!" he said. "Your heart is hard as iron – I have been wasting my breath. Nevertheless, pause before you act, in case the angry gods remember how you treated me, when your turn comes and you are brought down at the Scaean Gate in all your glory by Paris and Apollo."

'Death cut Hector short and his disembodied soul took wing for the House of Hades, bewailing its lot and the youth and manhood that it left. But Prince Achilles spoke to him again though he was gone. "Die!" he said. "As for my own death, let it come when Zeus and the other deathless gods decide."

'Then he withdrew his bronze spear from the corpse and laid it down.'*

This is 'approved' combat. It is not in the same category as the slaying of Abel. It is not approved because it is less bloody – it could hardly be more so, particularly when we remember the final desecration of Hector's body, dragged across the Trojan plain behind Achilles' chariot. It is approved because Hector has given offence to the gods. It is approved because Achilles is not acting on his own behalf, but as an instrument in the service of Pallas Athene. Achilles avoids the personal responsibility for Hector's death – a responsibility that would have put him in the same position as Cain – by acting not on his own behalf, but on behalf of a higher authority. Under this higher authority he is free to perpetrate any horror that occurs to him and still remain guiltless of it.

It seems that when the first man took up a stone club to strike down his neighbour there was a sense of shame in him that accompanied the action. He felt a sense of guilt at his behaviour. He needed to justify his action in terms of some higher authority who was directing him. And certainly this theme runs through the whole of human combat. The higher authority might be one of the gods, or when the gods had lost their

* *The Iliad* translated by E. V. Rieu. Penguin, 1950.

The personal equipment of the Roman legionary:
a life-size model in the Römisch-Germanisches
Zentralmuseum, Mainz.

The Roman auxiliary cavalryman attacking a
foot-soldier. A modern illustration in the Römisch-
Germanisches Zentralmuseum, Mainz.

potency as a concept, it might be an ideal of
'liberty' or 'freedom' or 'justice' or 'the State'.
But whatever that authority was, it relieved a man
of the personal responsibility of exercising the
supreme power – that of withdrawing life.

Xenophon, in his detailed account of the march
of the Ten Thousand into Persia in the early
fourth century BC, makes constant reference to
the same idea – the need to seek the opinion of
the gods before taking violent action, the need to
confirm that the final responsibility rested with
them and not with the men who were simply their
instruments. Professional soothsayers were employed for the purpose, divining from the appearance of sacrificed animals whether forthcoming combat had the support of the gods or not. The
idea is still current: modern armies are accompanied by padres who symbolise the support of
a deity, and so remove much of the individual
soldier's moral responsibility for his actions. Tacitus refers to a form of personal combat used by
some German tribes of the first century AD as a
form of augury in war-time. An enemy captive
was matched with a local champion, and from the
outcome the attitude of the gods to the forthcoming battle could be assessed.

This view of weapons as tools of the gods,
rather than of the men who were wielding them,
naturally endowed them with certain powers in
their own right. The tribes of Germany used them
to bind a marriage contract. Because of their
special powers, they conferred a solemnity on
such a contract that could not be conferred in any
other way. Similarly, the Macrones of Asia exchanged spears with Xenophon's Greeks as a sign
of the binding nature of their pledges. And the
magic quality of weapons and combat was the
central theme behind the dramatic dances of the
Paphlagonians and the tribes of Germany.

But besides the relationship that early man
saw between his fighting activities and some
deity, there was the relationship between the man
himself and the weapon he wielded. A weapon,
even in the early history of civilised man, was
never simply a piece of bronze or iron that he

picked up and used, something that was unrelated to himself. As we have seen, it was a tool he was using on behalf of some higher authority, it was something with a power to bind solemn agreements, it was something with a mystical power of its own. It bore the same relationship to him, surely, that a violin bears to a violinist. The violin is the instrument through which the violinist expresses part of himself – his musical insight. Similarly, a weapon is an instrument through which a man expresses his aggression, his courage, his physical prowess, his own individuality as a man. The fact that he needs to justify or legalise such expression in terms of a higher authority on whose behalf he is acting, or in terms of 'justice' or 'honour', in no way affects the basic truth – a weapon is an extension of the man using it. A similar view is expressed by John Lincoln in *One Man's Mexico* when, writing of the typical Mexican policeman, he talks of 'his legs straddling a powerful motor-bicycle in a stance which suggests that the roar from the exhaust is an audible extension of the sexual potency between his thighs'.* And the same view lies behind Tacitus' account of the funerals of famous men in first-century Germany. When a man died there, he was burned on a pyre; and since his weapons were as much a part of him as his body, they were burned with him. The weapon was, and still is, the man.

Similar ideas occur in later periods. T. H. White, retelling the Arthurian legend,† describes the drawing of the sword *Excalibur* from the anvil in which it was embedded:

'In the middle of the square there was a heavy stone with an anvil on it, and a fine new sword was stuck through the anvil.... "Come, sword," said the Wart. He took hold of the handles with both hands, and strained against the stone. There was a melodious consort on the recorders, but nothing moved. The Wart let go of the handles, when they were beginning

to bite into the palms of his hands, and stepped back, seeing stars.... He took hold of it again and pulled with all his might. The music played more strongly, and the light all about the churchyard glowed like amethysts; but the sword still stuck.'

Only when the Wart has invoked the magical powers of Merlyn is he prepared to try a third time:

'The Wart walked up to the great sword for the third time. He put out his right hand softly and drew it out as gently as from a scabbard.'

By his success, by demonstrating that he alone can draw the sword, he has established his kingship. The sword was destined to be drawn by him alone. It was *his* sword – a part of him. Magical powers prevented its possession by anyone but its true owner. Similarly, when the true owner of the sword is mortally wounded and can make no further use of it, it must be returned to the spirits from which it came. As the spirit of the King passes beyond this world, so does the sword which was part of him:

'Then Sir Bedivere departed, and went to the sword, and lightly took it up, and went to the water side, and there he bound the girdle about the hilts, and then he threw the sword as far into the water as he might, and there came an arm and an hand above the water, and met it, and caught it, and so shook it thrice and brandished, and then vanished away the hand with the sword in the water. So Sir Bedivere came again to the king, and told him what he saw. Alas, said the king, help me hence, for I dread me I have tarried over long.'*

Roland, no less anxious than King Arthur to prevent his sword *Durandal* from falling into other hands when defeat and death seemed imminent at the battle of Roncesvalles, tried to smash it

* *One Man's Mexico* by John Lincoln. The Bodley Head, 1967.

† *The Once and Future King* by T. H. White. Collins, 1958.

* *Morte d'Arthur* by Sir Thomas Malory, edited by Sir Edward Strachey. Macmillan, 1871.

to pieces on a rock. But such was the magic power of the sword that instead of splintering, it cleft open the rock itself.

Apart from these attitudes to weapons and to combat, attitudes which persist throughout history, what of the weapons themselves and the way they were used? The first metal to be used with real success in the manufacture of weapons was bronze. Hephaestus, working on the armour of Achilles, first 'cast it in imperishable bronze', then beat it and finally rubbed and polished it. The same techniques were used to produce sword-blades, axe- and spear-heads and knives. Yet bronze had its drawbacks. To produce a stiff blade of any length it was necessary to make it fairly thick. This added to the weight and cut down its manœuvrability. Bronze will take an edge – Agamemnon 'slit the lambs' throats with the relentless bronze and dropped them gasping to the ground' without apparent difficulty – but that edge is not particularly durable. It is easily blunted by contact with armour and with opposing weapons. These problems were not solved until the introduction of iron as the raw material out of which weapons were fashioned. And that introduction is perhaps the most important single development in the history of human combat. The material itself, coupled with the technique of forging instead of casting, meant the production of lighter weapons. It meant not only that future weapons would take a very sharp point and edge, but that point and edge would be durable. It meant that brass and bronze armour, which had previously been able to withstand blows from bronze weapons, would cease to give the same protection in future. Iron indeed produced a revolution. Tacitus, in his comments on first-century Germany, indicates how important a material it had by then become: 'There is not even any great abundance of iron, as may be inferred from the character of their weapons. Only a very few use swords or lances. They seldom use weapons of iron, but cudgels often.' And the cudgel was certainly no match for the Roman *gladius* forged of iron.

We have seen how Achilles used the weapons of 'unrelenting bronze'. The fight was purely individual, in the sense that Achilles was not dependent on widely accepted techniques that he had been taught. The moves he made were those that experience in battle had shown him were most suited to his own weapons and his own individual ability. He fought with superhuman vigour and passion. His fighting style required great physical strength, for when he struck Deucalion's neck with his sword he 'sent head and helmet flying off together'. He fought with savagery and utterly without compromise or compassion. He fought 'like a driving wind' and 'chased his victims with the fury of a fiend'. It was a style of fighting characteristic of a great deal of personal combat during the succeeding two thousand years. The fight with weapons of iron differed little from this, despite the enormous possibilities opened up by its discovery. Weight was still a virtue, since it lent impetus to any cutting stroke, and although the use of iron made it possible to produce a sword with a sharp point, the use of such a point was largely ignored. The spear, not the sword, was the weapon for thrusting.

The *gladius* of the Roman legionary was one of the exceptions to this. It was designed principally as a short thrusting sword for use with the *scutum*, the legionary's large, semi-cylindrical shield. Tacitus refers to this combination of *gladius* and *scutum* in use against the early British. The British were armed with small shields and large, unwieldy swords, 'swords without a thrusting point, and therefore unsuited to the clash of arms in close fighting'. The technique of the Batavi cohorts was to close in to sword-point, 'rain blow after blow, push with the bosses of their shields and stab at their enemies in their face'. Yet the Roman legionary was not really concerned with the kind of combat in which his personal skill alone could decide the issue. He fought as part of a mass formation – as part of a human tank – and his own success was very much dependent on the protection offered him by the shields and *gladii* of his comrades on either side.

Chapter Two

THE INDIVIDUALISTS

1

The Roman legionary and the Greek Hoplite fought as cogs in a machine. They were drilled and disciplined so as to fit instinctively into a pattern of mass attack in battle. True, if we were to isolate the activities of a single legionary in battle, we would see his individual behaviour and in this sense we could regard him as being engaged in personal combat. But his behaviour was much like that of his comrades, and he was dependent to a considerable extent on those comrades on either side of him for his own security.

There was one man, however, who did fight alone with *gladius* and *scutum*, and therefore does come within our terms of reference. The Samnite fought in the gladiatorial arenas equipped with the weapons of the legionary. His fight, as far as can be judged, was a good deal more active than that of the legionary, since he had no comrades at his side on whom he could rely for some protection. In his defence he was entirely dependent on his own individual skill. He took all blows aimed at him on his *scutum*, or else he relied on speed of movement to avoid them. In attack, he used the sharp point of the *gladius* for thrusting in the same manner as the legionary, but he also made use of the blade for cutting. So although the general description of personal combat of these days still holds good, the Samnite does constitute an important exception to it. Other gladiators seem equally to demonstrate other forms of personal combat – the Retiarius with his net and trident, the fully armed Secutor, the Thracians with small circular bucklers and large daggers – yet they are not typical of the period. They are, as it were, an interesting offshoot of the main development. Without question their combat was serious. Certainly it was personal. But few of these gladiators engaged in it out of choice. Most of them were prisoners of war, slaves or criminals under sentence of death. Where necessary, they were forced into the arena by hot irons or strokes of the whip. Their purpose in fighting was not to satisfy their own honour or to serve as divine instruments as did Achilles, but to provide a spectacle of blood for an insatiable audience. True,

1 Bronze statuette in the British Museum of a fully-armoured Roman gladiator.

2 The fighting technique of the Retiarius.

3 Sacrificial gladiatorial combat between Roman prisoners in front of the funeral pyre of a nobleman.

they were kept in 'schools', and no doubt certain theories and techniques of personal combat were worked out there. But it would be mistaken to regard such schools as in any way comparable with those of sixteenth-century Italy or of eighteenth-century England – places where men could freely study the exercise of arms as part of their total education. It is clear what kind of 'schools' these gladiators were kept in when we remember that the remains of one such establishment discovered at Pompeii revealed that many of them lived their lives in chains. The 'education' of a gladiator must have differed very little from the training of any other animal for combat in the arena.

The opponents of the Roman legionary – Germans, Britons, Franks, Picts – fought much more as individuals than did the legionary himself. This at least they had in common with the gladiators. They lacked the discipline – or perhaps refused it – that would have welded them into a coherent army, each man closely dependent on the next. We can perhaps safely conclude that the way they fought in battle was very much the same way in which they fought in personal combat. Indeed, to them battle was little more than innumerable personal combats taking place in a confined geographical location. With the gradual disintegration of the Roman empire, together with its disciplined fighting technique, this stress on combat as a personal and individual affair grew. 'We must remember', says Ellis Davidson, writing of the period, 'that battle for the Germanic peoples and the Vikings was a very individual affair. The picture of it which emerges from the comments of Greek and Latin historians and again from the poetry and sagas of the people themselves is principally one of single combat between sword-warriors, or a hand-to-hand struggle between two small bands of men.'*

The Viking warrior – certainly the man who formed part of a small, sea-borne raiding party – was a supreme individualist. His weapons were

* *Gods and Myths of Northern Europe* by H. R. Ellis Davidson. Penguin, 1964.

1 The individual nature of combat in the eleventh century. Scenes from the Bayeux Tapestry.

2 Caesar and Pompey fighting a duel on horseback, from a fourteenth-century French manuscript.

peculiarly his, unlike those of the Roman legionary whose *gladius* and *pila* were indistinguishable from those of a thousand of his comrades. The Viking might fight with the sword of his long-dead grandfather. He might fight with the re-hilted blade of a weapon brought to him by his wife as part of her dowry. He gave it a name – 'Drag-vandil', perhaps, or 'Hviting' – and so acknowledged that it had an individuality of its own. The spirit of that individuality might be reliable or unreliable. It might be a spirit that always allowed the weapon to be guided cleanly on to the target; alternatively, it might be a spirit that failed at the crucial moment and delivered the cut with the flat of the blade. It was a thing in itself, separate, complete, as unlike any other sword as the man who wielded it was unlike any other man. It was cherished, lest at the vital moment in combat it failed its owner. There were other weapons, equally endowed with individuality – the axe, the heavy spear, the short sax, the great round shield. Each had its own characteristics and its own personality. Such an attitude to weapons is perhaps understandable when we remember what was at stake if they failed a man, and the way in which the lives of many Northmen were almost exclusively orientated to their use.

The Viking *berserk* is perhaps in a category of his own. The Viking was, of course, supported by Odin in much the same way that Achilles had been supported by Pallas Athene. But the *berserk* seems to have been motivated by something more than this. His behaviour in battle, not so much fearless as totally careless about his own safety, has something in common with the astonishing activities of the Japanese *Kamikaze* pilot of the

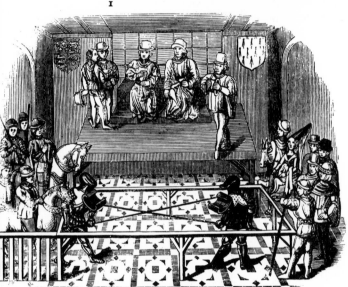

3 A tilting match on foot between two armoured men. Fifteenth century.

4 Varieties of jousting in the thirteenth century.

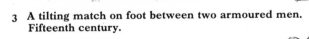

4

Second World War. We might regard him, rushing alone and stripped of his byrnie into the midst of an enemy mass, as not so much phenomenally brave as profoundly mad. Socially, he had something in common, too, with the gladiator of Rome. He was without property. He had nothing but his life to lose. He was largely outside the law. His end was usually bloody. Since he fought without compassion or quarter, he was given none. Hacked at with the broad-bladed swords of the enemy, rammed through with their spear-thrusts, he fell, finally dismembered with their axes. His frenzy in battle was terrifying to an opponent. If not actually caused by drink, then perhaps aggravated by it, it was a frenzy that we associate more usually with peoples less civilised than were the Vikings. We associate such a condition more with the war dances of primitive African tribes or with those of some North American Indians, than with any European warriors. Perhaps it had a similar motivation to the one that can still drive the entranced devotee of voodoo to seemingly superhuman acts. Whatever its cause, death alone could stop the *berserk* in full charge.

The Viking was principally a 'sword-warrior'. A glance at the fine collection of Viking swords in the Historical Museum in Oslo is sufficient to convince even the most non-specialist viewer that the popular idea of such weapons is quite inaccurate. They were neither particularly heavy nor – in practised hands – particularly cumbersome. The average weight was perhaps no more than two and a half pounds. The heavy pommel gave a certain balance to them. Granted, they were 'blade-heavy', but this is an advantage in a heavy cutting weapon. No particular attention was given to the production of a sharp point or to its use. This is logical enough when we remember that the enemy that the sword was designed to quell was usually clad in the byrnie – the over-garment of mail. A cut with such a sword would cleave its way through such a protection, or at least smash the limb beneath it, whereas penetration with the point would be much more difficult. The sax, since it was shorter than the sword, would be

particularly effective for thrusting upwards underneath the protection of the byrnie. A powerful thrust with the heavy spear – either thrown or held in the manner of a short lance – would penetrate the byrnie, whilst the axe would chop its way through anything – shield, helmet, byrnie and the bone beneath. Even the large circular shield, apart from its apparent use by the *berserk* as something on which he occasionally bit in the process of building up his frenzy, was used as a weapon of offence. The boss could be rammed straight into an opponent's face, or the edge could be used to deliver a crushing blow.

We can still see the essence of Viking combat in the Bayeux Tapestry. True, it is the southern Vikings of Normandy who are pictured, but they still wear the byrnie and their weapons are not significantly different from those used three centuries earlier in the Norse invasions of eastern England. The vigour and savagery of the combat is at once apparent, so is its personal quality. Here a swordsman chops down at the mailed shoulder of an axeman; next to him a man sways, a sword rammed clean through him at the lower border of his byrnie. A man falls from a sword-cut to the side of his head, whilst another has been beheaded by a similar stroke. One man has been struck completely off his feet by an upward axe-stroke. Another falls from a spear-thrust in the breast. The lower border of the tapestry is filled with unbelievable carnage. Yet there is a new factor here, the armoured horseman. Combat on horseback, of course, was by no means new. It had been in existence from much earlier times. Yet from the Norman horseman we might directly trace the rise of the heavily armoured knight of the period of 'chivalry'.

It was inevitable that the unbridled, individual combat of the Viking warrior should become systematised. A system was required that would put acceptable restrictions on the otherwise socially dangerous activities of the warrior – harness and canalise, as it were, the violent aggression out of which they rose. But a system that still allowed him to engage in martial exercise, approved his

The tournament in the sixteenth century.

A modern view of sword and buckler combat between mounted man and man on foot. From the film *The Red Mantle*.

use of arms, gave him opportunities for displays of personal courage and skill, and justified those activities in the name of Christendom, honour, justice, king and country. The system we know as 'chivalry' did all these things. Within it, and subject to certain stringent rules, personal combat was regarded as being one of the highest forms of human behaviour.

This formalising of personal combat under pressure of the needs of society has been traced to the early part of the fifth century AD, but as we have seen, many of its elements existed from the moment when the first man struck down his neighbour. Where chivalry differs from earlier systems is that it is a purely *Christian* system presided over by the Christian God. In it, dedication to the Christian Church, as opposed to a direct dedication to a particular god, plays a highly significant part. The Trial by Combat was a part of this new system, yet such trials had formed part of earlier combat. The Vikings, for example, accepted the outcome of such combat for legal purposes. The principle behind such combat was logical enough: since God was believed to approve the just use of arms, the outcome of a trial by combat must be just. God granted strength to the righteous and saw to it that he triumphed. In much the same way did Pallas Athene guide the hand of Achilles and hinder the activities of Hector. Inevitably such a form of trial was open to exceptions, and ultimately to corruption. A woman, for example, could hardly be expected to defend herself against an unjust accusation by taking up arms against an experienced warrior. Nor could a child. A man in his late sixties could hardly be expected to succeed in combat – though some in fact attempted it – with a virile young man in his twenties, however much support God might give him. It seems that there were laws even God could not offend against. In such cases a 'champion' – a stand-in – could be appointed, and the emergence of the professional champion tended to defeat the intention of the trial.

This professional champion, however, is an important person in the development of personal

1 **Mounted combat with swords in the late sixteenth century.**

2 **Armoured men at broadsword and dagger play on foot: late sixteenth century. From Segar's *Book of Honor and Armes*.**

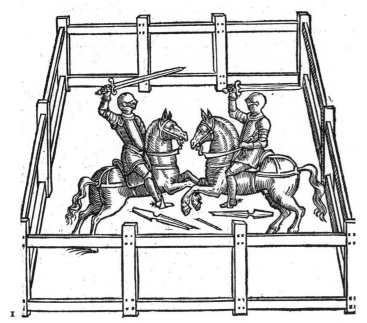

1

2

combat. Naturally, if he was a professional fighter, he could be expected to know more about personal combat than most other people. His advice was sought on combat matters. He was called in officially in some cases of trial by combat, to teach a prospective combatant some of the basic elements of play with the sword, the lance and other chosen weapons. He became in a way the first professional teacher of combat, and as such we can perhaps trace the start of coherent theories of personal combat to him.

But justice was not the only banner under which men fought one another in these formalised affairs. Honour was an equally sound excuse. Aspersions on the courage or honesty of a man were sufficient excuse for him to issue a challenge to single combat. The outcome either cleared his name or justified the accusations against him. It was this theme that dominated the duel in later years, the theme of personal honour.

If personal honour and justice were found on occasions to be insufficient excuse for personal combat, then Christendom itself could be invoked. 'He that hath no sword,' says St Luke, 'let him sell his garment, and buy one. . . . And they said, Lord, behold, here are two swords. And he said unto them, It is enough.' The theme, as we have seen, was a particularly telling one in the period of chivalry. It was the theme, after all, that set down many of the knights and armies of Europe – and a great deal of its wealth – in the Middle East during the protracted period of the Crusades. 'Most Holy Lord, Almighty Father,' runs Uden's translation of an inscription from the cathedral at Chartres, 'thou who hast permitted on earth the use of the sword to repress the malice of the wicked and defend justice . . . cause thy servant here before thee, by disposing his heart to goodness, never to use this sword or another to injure anyone unjustly; but let him use it always to defend the just and right.' It sums up much of the chivalrous attitude to arms. So does the *Decalogue* of Gautier, again quoted by Uden, laying down the ten principles of knightly conduct:

The use of the war hammer in combat on foot:
early seventeenth century. From Pistofilo's *Il
Torneo*.

1. Unswerving belief in the Church (no longer God himself, we may notice) and obedience to her teachings.

2. Willingness to defend the Church.

3. Respect and pity for all weakness and stead-fastness in defending them.

4. Love of country.

5. Refusal to retreat before the enemy.

6. Unceasing and merciless war against the infidel.

7. Strict obedience to the feudal overlord, so long as those duties did not conflict with duty to God.

8. Loyalty to truth and to the pledged word.

9. Generosity in giving.

10. Championship of the right and the good, in every place and at all times, against the forces of evil.

Sound enough principles in themselves, and oddly reminiscent of many of the Thirty-nine Articles of the Church of England – principles which still embody much of what we would regard today as the behaviour of a 'gentleman'. Yet, like all codes of chivalry, they were designed to impose some control on man's aggressive instincts. They were not, as has been suggested, designed to improve him as a fighting animal, to make him more courageous in combat, more fearless, more pugnacious. By nature he was already all those things. They were an attempt to canalise his native aggression into socially acceptable channels. To a considerable extent they succeeded.

Initially the fight still took place on foot. It was confined within a strict structure of rules and presided over by some authority. But as the procedure became increasingly formal, personal combat in this category usually began on horseback. The combatants were protected by an increasing amount of armour and in consequence their weapons were those that would break through that protection and penetrate the body inside. Alternatively they were weapons that would strike the armour covering with such force as to knock the man inside into insensibility. They relied on the lance for unseating an opponent. If this broke, they could use the sword, the flail or the axe in subsequent charges. Once dismounted, the opponent could be crushed insensible with the war hammer or mace, chopped apart with the axe or stabbed through the articulations of the armour with the large pointed sword. Confined within the rigid rules of such a combat, a man might still crave mercy when beaten to his knees and no longer able to defend himself. But to do so could condemn him to a future of shame. He might find himself no longer able to face his social peers. In such cases his end came with the misericorde, stabbed into his face through the open visor of his helmet or thrust into him through some gap in the articulations of his armour.

For such occasions he practised, alone with the quintain both mounted and on foot, with colleagues and men more proficient than himself. He put such practice to the test in the formal tournament, on the pretext of fitting himself for service under the king or a feudal overlord. Uden describes the tournament as 'the chief sport and most important training school of the age of chivalry; the training ground of the great warrior, the opportunity for the unknown and fortuneless, the career of the landless, the favourite spectacle of the masses. They began as real encounters with dangerous weapons, in which a man hazarded life and limb, and finished as more-or-less harmless pageants.

Yet training in this formal kind of personal combat, with its trumpet fanfares, its patrons, its spectacle and apparent glamour, was still largely through experience. Little material exists to suggest a regularised training process involving an understanding of certain basic principles and of the techniques arising out of them. There was no coherent theory of personal combat that guaranteed success to the skilled man over an opponent relying on brute force. The strong man, the durable man, the man who could ride hardest and best take the punishment dealt out to him by the weapons of his opponent, was the winner. This was the period of pre-theory. It needed a revolution to change its combat techniques.

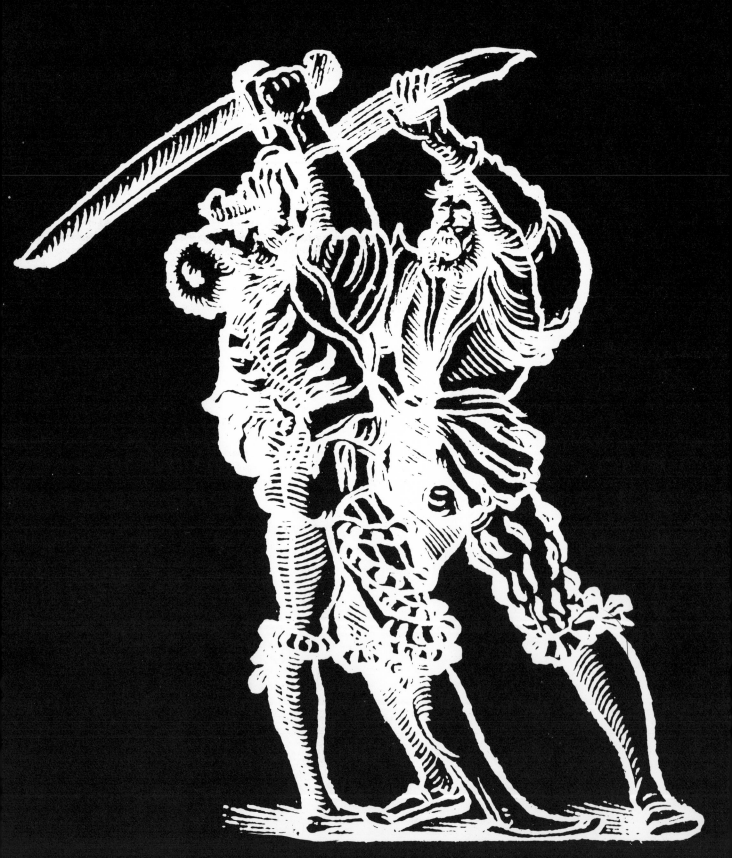

Chapter Three

THE ASCENDANCY OF THE SWORD

'Paradoxical as it seems,' says Egerton Castle, 'the development of the "Art of Fence"* was the result of the invention of firearms.'† There is a good deal of truth in his statement. The principal development during the earlier part of the Middle Ages had been the improvement in body armour. The mail byrnie of the Vikings had been sufficient to give reasonable protection to the fighting man from the sword-blows of his adversary, whilst leaving him with a certain freedom of movement. But the byrnie could not withstand solid blows with the axe, nor could it withstand the impact of the arrow as Hastings and Crécy had shown. The logical answer to the improvement of weapons was to increase body armour. Mail was replaced by plate, and thin plate by thicker. The result was the fully armoured man, carrying some sixty pounds of sheet metal on the surface of his body. When he fought mounted, he had a certain mobility still, but when he fought on foot that mobility was considerably restricted.

Increased defence has always produced new weapons designed to overcome it. The period of heavy personal armour was accompanied by the development of weapons that would crack it or slip through its articulations to penetrate the human body inside. The war hammer, the mace, the axe and poleaxe, the morning star and flail, all fall into this first category. The misericorde dagger and a new type of thrusting sword both fall into the second.

It was this concept of personal defence by heavy armour that the firearm shattered. It was theoretically possible at this time to produce armour of sufficient thickness to withstand the blows of the armour-cracking weapons – though such armour would have reduced the mobility of the wearer to nil. But it was not possible to produce personal armour of sufficient thickness to withstand the blow of a missile impelled by a charge of gunpowder. At one blow, the theory of

* Although 'fence' is a contraction of 'defence', the 'Art of Fence' referred to by Castle includes the use of arms for attack as well as for defence.
† *Schools and Masters of Fence* by Egerton Castle. George Bell, 1885.

Falchion fighting as taught by Lebkommer in the early sixteenth century. From *Der Allten Fechter*. (See also page 32.)

personal defence through heavy body armour fell apart. In consequence, those weapons specifically designed to answer that particular method of defence became redundant. With the severe reduction in the weight of body armour, mobility returned, and against mobility the mace, the hammer and the morning star were of little use. The participant in personal combat was thrown back very largely on the sword and on certain staff weapons. Energy that had previously been spent on designing new methods of cracking armour, was now diverted to considerations of new methods of using the sword.

Fortunately, perhaps, skill with the sword had not fallen into abeyance during the period of armour. To arm for the lists was an expensive business and there were many who could afford no more than a shirt of mail. The archer at Agincourt, for example, was not clad in plate. In personal combat he still relied on the sword. So did the apprentice in the larger towns of Europe. For defence such men relied on agility and on the buckler, very much as men had done for five hundred years and more. There was here a continuous tradition of sword and buckler play, but it was a tradition that relied very much on personal tricks and personal ability. It was not a tradition that had thrown up any systematic practice or theory.

But now the old trial-and-error process was injected with new blood. Those noblemen who could no longer rely on the safety of armour had to turn to the sword. They needed education in its use, and much of the available education they found unsatisfactory. Pressure from them produced a new race of Masters – no longer simply the professional champions and travelling gladiators of the earlier period, but men who had considered the nature and possibilities of the weapon and had made some attempt to build up coherent theories concerning its use.

In England, during the early sixteenth century, the position of the professional Master of Defence – the professional teacher of the art of arms – was scarcely one which would have produced the answer to this new demand. True, by the middle of the fifteenth century it was probably safe for a man to admit that he ran a school of fence, though legislation of the thirteenth and fourteenth centuries forbidding such schools was still in force. But the professional fencing teacher was still classed with 'rogues and vagabonds' – and actors! – and such a classification did not encourage lively, analytical and discriminating minds into the profession.

In Italy, Germany and Spain the situation was much better. The Master of Arms had a special place in society. He could teach his art, and he was regarded as an authority in matters of honour. As early as the fourteenth century, the German masters had formed the *Bürgerschaft von St Marcus von Löwenberg* – the association of *Marxbrüder* – in Frankfurt am Main, which gave them a monopoly over the teaching of the use of arms, and the Germans can claim what appears to be the earliest extant book of fence – Hans Lebkommer's *Der Altenn Fechter an fengliche Kunst*. There is evidence to suggest that prior to the sixteenth century the German fighting man was more efficient in handling the two-handed sword, the sword and buckler and the *Düsack*, than any other man in Europe.

And yet the first coherent system of handling the sword in personal combat appeared in Italy. Marozzo – a Bolognese with a school in Venice – published his *Opera Nova* in 1536, and in it gives a good idea of what personal combat was like in the late fifteenth and early sixteenth centuries. The sword was gripped with one or two fingers round the *quillons* – the cross-guard. It could be used alone, or more usually with the buckler or the target held in the left hand for defence. As the illustrations show, the 'guards' of Marozzo varied considerably and to a modern eye have no particular coherence. They do not actually *guard* anything, in the sense that if a fighter adopts any one of them he can still be hit almost anywhere on his body unless he moves or strikes the attacking weapon aside. They are merely positions from which the fighter might launch an attack, or

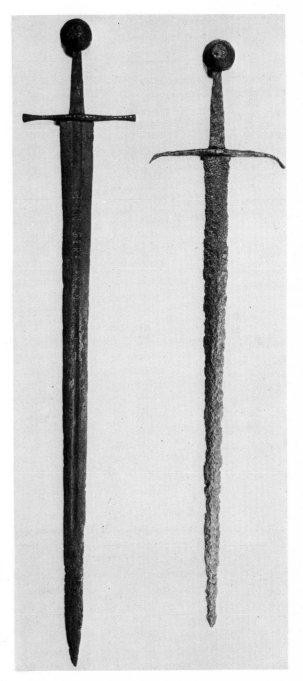

defend himself with a counter-attack.

The weapon that Marozzo had in mind was heavy and ill-balanced, still with traces of its armour-cracking forebears. It had a simple, straight cross-guard (the *quillons*) and semi-circular additions below the guard (the *pas d'âne* rings of later weapons) to protect the fingers. An additional finger protection may have existed in the form of a semi-circular piece of metal linking the *pas d'âne* at their base, over the blade. The section of blade within the *pas d'âne* (the *ricasso* of later weapons) was squared so as not to cut the fingers. The blade – the length of which varied according to the user – was double-edged and pointed. Because of the lack of adequate protection that such a weapon gave to the hand, it was used in conjunction with a heavy mailed gauntlet. (As was the habit with many early theorists on the use of the sword, the one shown in Marozzo's illustrations is not typical of the period.)

Pupils of Marozzo paid considerable attention to the use of both edges of the blade for cutting an opponent. Cuts were delivered from the right (against the opponent's left side) – the *mandritti* – and from the left – *roversi*. They could be delivered horizontally, vertically upwards or downwards, or obliquely – the *tondo, montante, fendente* and *sgualembrato*. They could be delivered with either the right edge or the false edge of the blade. Curiously, although the weapon was pointed, Marozzo makes little reference to its use in this way, although his illustrations make it quite clear that thrusting was part of his teaching. The play was in fact cut and thrust broadsword play, characteristic of the earlier period.

For his defence, the fighter produced by Marozzo's teaching might do one of three things. He might dodge an attack altogether, either by ducking, in the case of an attack on his head, or by stepping backwards or to one side. He might meet the opponent's blade on his buckler – secured to his left forearm – or target – held by a single handgrip, or ward it off with a cloak wrapped twice round his left forearm, or with his left hand protected by a mailed glove. Finally, he could

Marozzo's positions for the fight with the sword and hand buckler.

defend himself with his sword by launching a counter-attack at the same moment as his opponent's sword moved towards him. The counter-attack would not only force the opposing blade out of the way; it would also continue forwards and strike the opponent. Such a counter-attack with the point would be aimed at the face. Even a minor blow there could be debilitating; equally, it was still by no means unusual for fighters to wear mail shirts as a protection against thrusts to the body.

We can imagine a personal combat conducted according to such teaching. Each fighter came on guard in any one of the eleven positions described by Marozzo. The point of each sword would almost certainly be threatening the face of the opponent, the hand might be high or low, depending on whether a fighter took up the *guardia di faccia* or the *cinghiara porta di ferro*. The fighter might stand with either foot advanced, the weight resting over it. The buckler or target he would hold before him, in most cases in a position to

protect the head. The fighters would begin the combat out of distance, changing guards to test the reactions of the opponent, looking constantly for an opening through which to deliver a cut. They would move round one another, anti-clockwise, hoping to 'gain' a position from which they could more safely launch an attack on the opponent's left side and away from his sword-arm.

When an opening appeared at last, the attack would be launched 'on the pass', that is, by advancing the back foot past the forward one and so closing the distance between the two fighters by some three or four feet. As the distance closed, the protagonist would cut at some exposed part of his opponent. It might be downwards on his head, with a *mandritta sgualembrato*, or under his buckler at his advanced left thigh with a *mandritta tondo*. He might, alternatively, cut with the false edge at an exposed knee or wrist.

The defendant could step backwards to avoid the attack and at the same time thrust at his opponent's face. Or he could parry the attack with

Various guards according to Marozzo. From *Opera Nova*.

1 The guard with the sword and large buckler.

2 With the sword and dagger.

3 The guard for the man armed with two swords.

4 With the sword and cloak.

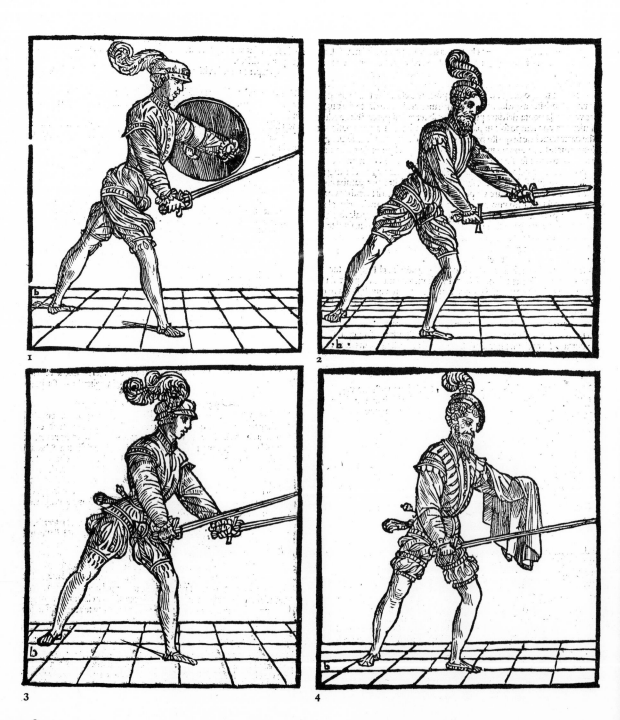

his buckler and again deliver a thrust in the face as he did so. Equally, he might decide to meet the oncoming blade with his own sword, deflecting it from its target and at the same time thrusting with his own point at the enemy.

The whole fight was energetic, with a good deal of general movement – passing, slipping to one side, changing guards, having first the right foot forward and then the left. Strength and endurance were essential qualifications for success. We should remember, too, that two men meeting in earnest would not feel restricted by any rules of gentlemanly conduct. All the rough-and-tumble techniques of the earlier periods were still legitimate in serious combat. Wrestling, tripping and kicking were all legitimate moves. The cloak could could be tossed over the opponent's sword, or thrown over his face, and the move followed by an immediate attack on him. In the case of a fight with the sword alone, the opponent's weapon could be grasped by the blade with the mailed left hand, or it could be seized by the guard and torn from his grasp in what is delicately called a 'disarm'. In considering personal combat of this period – and indeed of many later periods – we should dismiss from our minds any idea we have of modern fencing. When two men met, bent on doing one another to death, they did not consider such niceties as rules and regulations. There was only one rule – success – and anything that contributed to it was acceptable.

Manciolini and Marozzo were fighting men. They taught the art of dispatching an opponent with the sword and with the other weapons of the day. They were practitioners, and as such they dealt with those moves that experience had taught them were most effective. Unlike them, Agrippa was not a teacher of fence, though he clearly had a good deal of practice in the use of the sword. He was essentially a theorist – a mathematician, engineer and architect – who applied principles of logic to the use of the sword. He was a simplifier of the complexities of Marozzo. The eleven guards of Marozzo he reduced to four. This was not merely a simplification, it also produced more

logical positions. The guards of Marozzo were obviously those that Marozzo had found by experience to be most useful for himself. Out of that personal experience he had taught a system. But Agrippa was able to detach himself from his experience and attempt to deduce principles which would be more widely applicable. His *prima guardia*, with the hand above the head and the point of the sword aimed at the opponent, is one that a swordsman falls into naturally in the act of drawing. As the weapon is drawn from the scabbard, the sword-hand rises. Only when the hand is above and in front of the head, is the point of the weapon clear of the scabbard. To reach Agrippa's *prima guardia* from this position, requires no more than the direction of the sword-point towards the opponent.

For Agrippa's *seconda guardia* the hand is lowered from above the head to shoulder level. A further drop of the hand to a position a little outside the right hip brings the fighter into Agrippa's *terza guardia*, and his final guard – *quarta* – is similar, but with the hand outside the left hip. All these guards are still no more than attitudes from which a move might be launched; they still do not 'guard' anything. But they must have been a considerable improvement on Marozzo's guards for the Italian tyro of the mid-sixteenth century. Even the names are a considerable advance: *terza guardia* is a good deal easier to remember than Marozzo's *guardia di coda lunga e stretta*.

In a sense, Agrippa might be regarded as the man who defined the rapier as a weapon that could be used effectively for thrusting as well as cutting, since he mentions the use of the point of the sword in a way that indicates he attached importance to the move, a thrust forward from the shoulder at face or breast, with the sword-arm extended. Marozzo regarded the sword as principally a cutting weapon that could on occasion be used for thrusting. Agrippa regards it as a weapon in which the point was at least equal in importance to the edge. Indeed, the rapier of the mid-sixteenth century already shows this change in attitude from the time of Marozzo. Its balance had improved, which, making it less blade-heavy, increased its thrusting potential whilst at the same time slightly reducing its effectiveness in the cut. The guard of the weapon grew more complex. Side-rings appeared on one or both sides of the *quillons*, giving additional protection to the hand. In some cases, counter-curving of the *quillons* appeared producing an early form of knuckle-bow which gave additional protection to the outside of the fingers. Agrippa's illustrations show that the dagger, held in the left hand, was largely replacing the target and buckler of Marozzo's age.

We cannot say that the theories of Agrippa necessarily influenced those of Grassi, since their two publications were no more than two years apart – 1568 and 1570. But certainly the methods of the two have much in common. Both men were simplifiers of Marozzo's complexities, both had a logical and systematic approach to the business of personal combat. Grassi further reduced the number of guards with the sword to three, corresponding roughly to the *prima*, *seconda* and *terza guardia* of Agrippa, though these remained no more than attitudes from which to initiate a movement. He goes further in his analysis of sword-play than Agrippa, classifying the blade into four parts. The two quarters nearer the guard he recommends for parrying, the third quarter is to be the part with which the cut is made, and the fourth quarter is reserved for thrusting. And on the matter of thrusting, he refines Agrippa's ideas further, by stating that he regards the thrust as being more effective than the cut. If we can regard Agrippa as the originator of the rapier, then we might regard Grassi as the precursor of the small sword of the eighteenth century.

He analysed, too, the four areas in which attacks might be made, as high, low, inside and outside. The high and low lines are defined as being above or below an imaginary line drawn horizontally through the body at about the level

The positions recommended by Marozzo for the fight with the single sword.

The guard recommended by Marozzo for the sword and cloak man when facing a mounted opponent.

The four guards of Agrippa. From *Trattato.*

Figura per il Cap. IIII.

Figura per il Cap. V.

Figura per il Cap. VII.

Figura per il Cap. VII.

Agrippa's positions in action.

of the bottom of the rib cage. The inside and outside lines lie to a fighter's left and right of an imaginary line drawn vertically through his own body. Grassi's 'outside' guard, then – the *guardia largha* – was one in which the fighter held the hilt of his sword to the right of this imaginary vertical line.

Grassi speaks of the dagger as if it was the best defensive arm for use with the rapier. Certainly the movement of the time was in this direction. The cloak was still in use, and, when properly used, was effective against both cuts and thrusts. It was wrapped twice round the left forearm and a piece of it allowed to trail below the arm. This piece was opposed to an oncoming cut in such a way as to take the force out of it. Against the thrust the point was either enveloped by the material and swept aside, or it penetrated the material and so became enmeshed in it. Grassi is at pains to point out that in using the cloak the left leg should not be advanced behind it. The result of ignoring such advice would be the skewering of one's cloak to one's own left leg by the opponent's point! The buckler was still used with the rapier, held out well in front of the body to offer the maximum defence, but it is clear that with the gradual lightening of the rapier the dagger became its most regular companion.

The 'case of rapiers' had recently come into use, following the pair of similar weapons that Marozzo had mentioned. On the face of it, it might appear clumsy and ineffective to pair the rapier in the right hand with another in the left – instead of with a dagger or buckler. But it was the practice to encourage students to be ambidextrous in using the rapier, even at times changing hands during a bout. So despite adverse comments by some modern authors, the case of rapiers in practised hands must have been formidable.

Finally, the theory and practice of rapier play in Italy during the third quarter of the sixteenth century was furthered by the book by Viggiani which appeared in 1575. Viggiani was a contemporary of Agrippa's and must have been intimately acquainted with the work of Marozzo.

The three 'wards' recommended by Grassi. From
True Arte of Defence.

1 **The high ward (left) and low ward.**

2 **The broad ward.**

1

2

He crystallises three points mentioned but not developed by Agrippa. He insists on the superiority of the thrust over the cut, and goes into some detail regarding the classification of various thrusts in much the same way as Marozzo had classified the cuts. He taught guards in which the right foot was always in front of the left, so leaving the way clear for the discarding of the dagger and for that sideways stance of the body which reduces the area of the target open to the opponent and characterises all later duelling with the sword. Where Agrippa had talked of thrusting from the shoulder, Viggiani develops this idea into the 'lunge'. The *punta sopramano*, as he calls his version of the lunge, is delivered by advancing the right foot with the sword-arm fully extended at the opponent's chest, at the same time counterbalancing this movement forward by lowering the left arm backwards. Even in the eighteenth century the movement had hardly developed beyond this point.

Between them, then, the Italian theorists and practitioners of the sixteenth century had carried the art of personal combat with the sword a long way. The gymnastic play with broadsword and buckler, characteristic of the fifteenth century and the earlier part of the sixteenth, had given way to a coherent system of fighting with the rapier. The cutting of the broadsword, accompanied by wrestling, tripping, striking in the face with the pommel, kneeing in the groin and blinding with tossed-up earth, had all been seen to be less effective in the business of killing a man than a single thrust with a rapier blade through face, chest or belly.

Chapter Four

CUT OR THRUST?

The sixteenth century saw the establishment of Italian theory and practice in personal combat as supreme. Yet the Italians were not the only Europeans interested in killing one another. The Germans had already established a reputation for providing men of the highest ability in the handling of a wide range of personal weapons. The *Marxbruder* was skilled in the use of the sword and buckler, the Zweyhänder, the braquemar and the halberd. He was in most cases an experienced fighting man – a practitioner – and he was in demand outside Germany as a teacher of combat.

Indeed, such was the influence of the German man of arms in the earlier part of the sixteenth century that the first extant book on the subject, published in French, seems very much to follow German practice. It contains nothing that we would recognise as rapier fighting, but deals with a range of cutting weapons with which the Germans were masters. It gives a clear idea of the violence that characterised the way in which they were used. It mentions wrestling and tripping as part of personal combat with the sword. It mentions the way in which the right knee may be driven into an opponent's groin when he has been thrown to the ground.

Sainct Didier, writing in 1573, tacitly acknowledges the supremacy of Italian theory and practice even in France. The terms he uses are 'frenchified', but they are used to describe moves already established by Marozzo, Agrippa and Grassi. He advocates three guards – a high, a middle and a low – which correspond closely to those already defined by the Italians. He mentions various positions that might be adopted by the left arm when fighting with the sword alone, and in this anticipates by two years the much more precise use of the left arm described by Viggiani in executing the *punta sopramano*. The modern practice in duelling of keeping the left arm well out of the way all the time is clearly only possible with a weapon light enough to be used for defence as well as for attack. In Sainct Didier's day the sword was still principally an

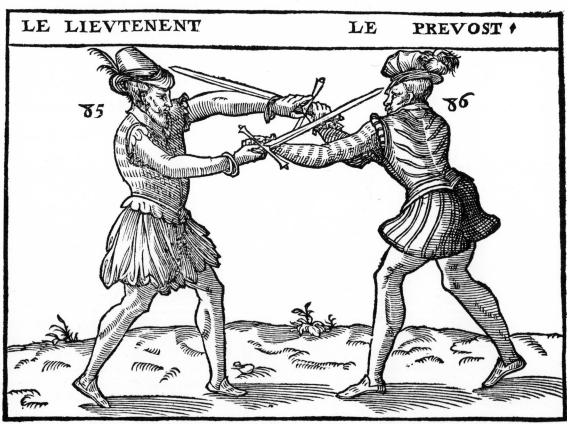

The disarm by seizing the opponent's guard and the
counter-seizure as a defence against the disarm.
From Sainct Didier's *Traicté*.

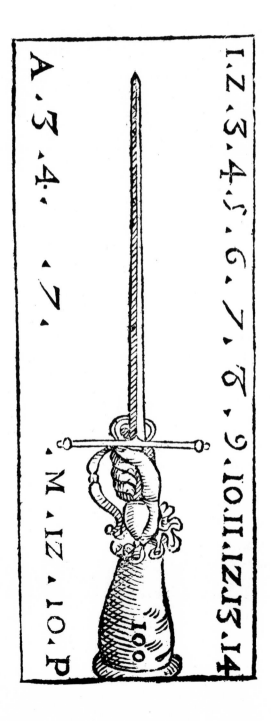

The weapon discussed by Carança. From *De la filosofia.*

arm of attack, since its weight did not allow that speed of movement necessary for its use as the sole means of defence as well. In consequence, the left hand had still a considerable part to play in that defence.

Sainct Didier classifies three ways of hitting an opponent, by *maindraicts* and *renvers* – the *mandritti* and *roversi* of Marozzo – and by *estocs* – thrusts with the point. In putting the *estoc* on a par with the cuts from right and left he is no further advanced than Agrippa. Indeed, his attempt to argue that the cut is more effective than the thrust puts him no nearer rapier play than was Marozzo.

Grassi had almost defined the *parry* with the sword as a definite move in itself. He had talked of the actual engagement of blades and suggested that the 'feel' of an opponent's blade might give one important clues as to how he was likely to use it, and this at a time when sword-blades in combat rarely touched, and then only when one was beaten aside by the other. Sainct Didier makes no mention of such ideas. To him the only way in which the sword might be used defensively was when it was launched as a counter-attack on an opponent's attack in such a way that it would deflect the attacking blade and at the same time strike the opponent. Such a move was well known to Marozzo and to the German practitioners of the previous century.

Like all exponents of early sword-play, Sainct Didier has his own ways of seizing an opponent's sword and wrenching it from his grasp. He describes, for example, a double seizure which results in the exchange of weapons. His Lieutenant – one of the two characters in Sainct Didier's book who explain his methods – advances his right foot towards his opponent – the Prevost – and thrusts. The Prevost withdraws his left foot, parries the opposing weapon, immediately advances his left foot and seizes the Lieutenant's sword at the grip. At the same time he threatens the Lieutenant's face with his point. The Lieutenant sways to his right to avoid the Prevost's point, advances his left foot and seizes the

1   The Spanish sword opposing the Turkish weapon.

2   The Spanish preoccupation with the circular form.

3   Plan view of the foot positions and the combat circle typical of Spanish swordfighting. From Narvaez' *Libro*.

Prevost's sword. The situation is now stalemate. In order to continue the fight each man relinquishes his own weapon and retains his opponent's. The exchange of weapons in the final scene of *Hamlet* might have come about by just such a move.

It is not surprising that Italian theory should already have shown such influence in other parts of Europe. The English gentleman made the Grand Tour to broaden his experience. The Frenchman visited the schools of fence in Bologna and Venice, and was naturally sensitive to the new ideas developing there. But what is surprising, as Castle points out, is that French theory and practice at this period should have lagged behind Italian, considering the French obsession with personal combat: 'The latter half of the sixteenth century saw, with the disuse of the judicial duels, the rise of that extraordinary mania for private duelling which cost France in 180 years the useless loss of 40,000 valiant gentlemen, killed in single combats which arose generally on the most futile grounds.'

The country least affected by these new Italian ideas was Spain. The reason is not obvious. There are references to the ability of the Spaniard as an individual fighting man that make it quite clear that he had as much interest in personal combat as any other European. Perhaps, since Spain is a peninsula, access to the rest of Europe was not quite so easy as for the Frenchman and the German. Or perhaps the pride of the Spaniard made him less susceptible to outside influence than others were. Whatever the reason, there grew up at this time a school of Spanish fencing which had a character all its own, and it was a style that ran continuously into the eighteenth century, hardly affected at all by developments elsewhere.

The names which dominate Spanish sword-play of the late sixteenth century, and continued to dominate it for two centuries and more, are Hieronimo de Carança and Don Luys Pacheco de Narvaez. Carança's *De la Philosofia de las Armas* first appeared in 1569. Narvaez – a pupil of Carança's – issued his *Libro de las Grandezas de la Espada* some thirty years later. Both works

1

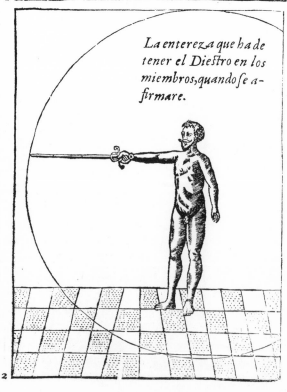

La entereza que ha de tener el Diestro en los miembros, quando se afirmare.

2

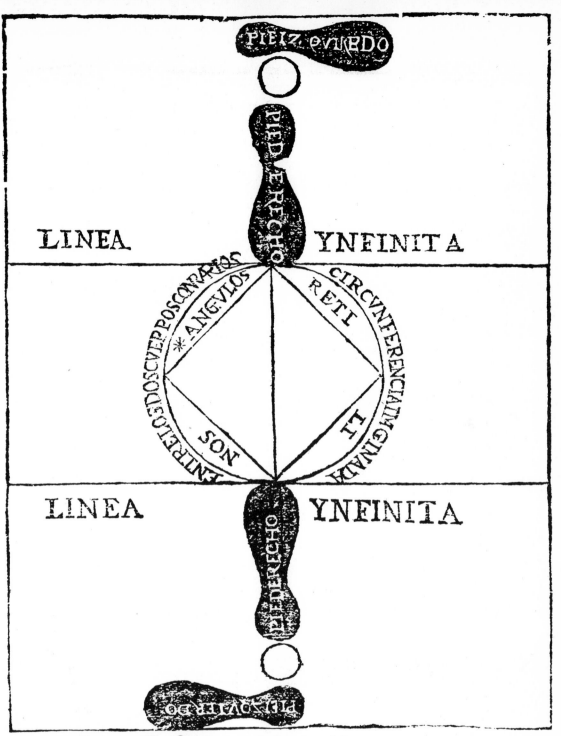

LINEA   YNFINITA

LINEA   YNFINITA

L Sabio artifice que a cargo toma hazer algun edificio, para que fea perfecto, firme y durable, pone fumo cuydado en facar los cimientos de la hõdura y entrañas de la tierra: y con fuma diligencia, con regla, y

E 4   otro

Play with the two-handed sword. From
Lebkommer's *Der Allten Fechter*.

1 Düsack play. From Sutor's *Künstliches Fechtbuch.*

2 Düsack play. From Meyer's *Gründliche Beschreibung.*

assume a knowledge of mathematics and philosophy. This in itself is not untypical of the period.
Other writers in other countries had frequently
prefaced their works with philosophical pro-
nouncements, as if in the matter of killing a man
there were universal principles involved, principles laid down in heaven to which the professional
fighting man had special access. But what is
particularly distinctive about Spanish theory is
the lengths to which this philosophising was
carried. As Castle comments: 'It is a remarkable
fact that in Spain, the supposed birthplace of
systematic swordsmanship, so little progress
should have been made towards what may be
called the more *practical* use of the sword. Whilst
the Italians and, after their example, the French,
Germans and English gradually discovered that
simplification led to perfection, the Spanish
masters, on the contrary, seemed to aim at making
fencing a more and more mysterious science, re-
quiring for its practice a knowledge of geometry
and natural philosophy, and whose principles
were only explainable on metaphysical grounds.'
This esoteric quality, this mystery, lies at the
back of all Spanish sword-play, and it seems even
to have influenced the use of the sword in modern
bullfighting. Whereas the Italians saw sword-play
as technique, the Spaniards saw it as ritual, a
kind of deadly dance in which the fighters were
in close contact with the essential mystery of life
and the immutable laws of the metaphysical
universe.

The illustrations – and particularly those from
the work of Thibault who followed the Spanish
school in the seventeenth century – give an idea
of the complexity of the system. A swordsman
came on guard in an erect position, out of distance of his opponent, his sword-arm fully extended, his weapon pointing directly at the
enemy. The right foot was a little in advance of the
left, so that the body was placed sideways on to
the enemy. The fight was conceived as taking
place within a circle and the *ganando los grados al
perfil* – a circular walk anti-clockwise round an
opponent until a position suitable for attack had

Fighting with the halberd and practice with the
two-handed sword in the German fencing school.
From Meyer's *Gründliche Beschreibung*.

The guard with the halberd. From Agrippa's *Trattato*.

been reached – was much favoured. The method of attack was to close the distance between oneself and one's opponent, by advancing with short steps along one of the chords of the circle; constantly menacing the enemy with one's point. A delivery with the point was made not with the *punta sopramano* of Viggiani, but by a simple stabbing movement. The point, in fact, was not regarded as being of particular importance. The play was principally concerned with cuts, delivered from the shoulder, the elbow or the wrist. Parries with the sword were seen always as counter-attacks, in the same way that Marozzo had seen them.

Yet there was one great virtue of the Spanish method. It insisted on great calm, calculation and coolness in combat. If the system of Carança did no more than collect together the best-known moves of the day and embed them in a mysterious philosophy, at least this insistence on cool deliberation produced swordsmen who were renowned throughout Europe as formidable duellists. Perhaps it was that the system, because of its complexity, was difficult to learn. To learn it required dedication and long hours of practice. And practice with the sword is perhaps more useful than any system.

Whatever the shortcomings of the system evolved by Carança and developed by Narvaez, it lasted almost unchanged in Spanish swordplay into the eighteenth century. And, since it unquestionably produced fine swordsmen, it must have had virtues that are no longer immediately apparent to us. It was certainly well known in England, as were the names of its two principal exponents, if we are to judge from Ben Jonson's play *The New Inne*:

Fly : Go by, Hieronymo.
Tip : What was he?
Fly : The Italian
That play'd with abbot Antony i' the Fryers,
And Blinkin-sops the bold.
Tip : I marry, those
Had fencing names, what's become o' them?

Host : They had their times, and we can say, they were. So had Caranza his: so had Don Lewis.
Tip : Don Lewis of Madrid is the sole master Now of the world.

We must not imagine, in the face of all this attention being given to rapier play during the later stages of the sixteenth century, that the rapier was the only tool for killing a man in personal combat. Meyer, writing in Germany in 1570, and developing the earlier work of Lebkommer, deals systematically with the use of the *Düsack*, the two-handed sword, the halberd and the flail. The *Düsack*, as the illustrations from Sutor's work show, was a particularly simple weapon in design, and may be classified with the anlace, braquemar and Landsknecht's sword, as a short cutting weapon. The *Düsack*, indeed, was exclusively a cutting weapon, and play with it required more than anything a good deal of general agility. Attacks were met with counter-attacks, rather than parries. The play was accompanied by all the rough and tumble that we associate with early cutting weapons. Defence was very much a question of dodging an opponent's attack.

The German two-hander might be better regarded as a staff weapon than as a sword, although a good deal more deadly than the quarterstaff. The weapon is easier to handle than examples on the walls of museums suggest. The balance is by no means poor, and when held with the right hand just above the cross-guard and the left hand on the pommel, the blade can be made to move with some rapidity and force. The action of the hands in two-hander play was rather like using a large pair of garden shears where one handle is a foot shorter than the other. The hands moved in opposite directions about an imaginary fulcrum set half-way between them. There were guards with the two-hander in the same way as there were with the sword. The blade could be used to parry, though dodging and the counter-attack were more usual methods of defence. The length

53

1

1 The trip with the halberd.

2 Fighting with the flail.

3 The sword opposed to the spiked flail. The scabbard in the swordsman's left hand is used defensively in place of the dagger.

4 Staff fighting. From Sutor's *Künstliches Fechtbuch.*

5 The guard with the English quarterstaff. From Swetnam's *Schoole of Defence.*

6 Staff fighting. From Meyer's *Gründliche Beschreibung.*

2

3

of the weapon could be shortened by moving the left hand from the pommel and grasping the blade below the cross-guard. At this point the blade had no edge and the hand was protected by a short secondary guard between it and the point. In this shortened position, the weapon could be used for stabbing in the same way as the modern rifle and bayonet.

Play with the halberd and flail was no less energetic than play with the two-hander. The halberd is the more interesting of the two weapons, since it can thrust as well as cut, whilst the flail is exclusively a cutting weapon – if we can use that word to describe the clubbing and crushing blows that the flail could inflict. Both weapons – and indeed the two-handed sword as well – could be used to deliver butt-strokes in the manner of modern rifle and bayonet fighting, and both could be used at varying lengths according to the position of the hands on the shaft.

German rapier play was a development of the Italian. The system was thorough but derivative. The illustrations from Meyer's book give a clear idea of how it was practised, and also the quality of determination and dedication behind that practice.

And of rapier play in England at the end of the sixteenth century we have the description given of it in *Romeo and Juliet*:

Prince: Benvolio, who began this bloody fray?
Benvolio: Tybalt here slain, whom Romeo's hand
   did slay,
  Romeo that spake him fair, bid him bethink
  How nice the quarrel was, and urg'd withal
  Your high displeasure: all this uttered,
  With gentle breath, calm look, knees humbly
   bow'd
  Could not take truce with the unruly spleen
  Of Tybalt deaf to peace, but that he tilts
  With piercing steel at bold Mercutio's breast,
  Who all as hot, turns deadly point to point,
  And with a martial scorn, with one hand beats
  Cold death aside, and with the other sends
  It back to Tybalt, whose dexterity
  Retorts it: Romeo he cries aloud,
  Hold friends, friends part, and swifter than
   his tongue,
  His agile arm beats down their fatal points,
  And 'twixt them rushes, underneath whose
   arm,
  An envious thrust from Tybalt, hit the life
  Of stout Mercutio, and then Tybalt fled,
  But by and by comes back to Romeo,
  Who had but newly entertain'd revenge,
  And to't they go like lightning, for ere I
  Could draw to part them, was stout Tybalt
   slain . . .

England, like Germany, was in two minds. The traditional weapons were the broadsword and buckler, yet the English were not unaware of the rapier. Contact with Italy during the century had been considerable. To the English upper classes, Italy was a kind of Mecca. They travelled there.

Staff fighting. From Lebkommer's *Der Allten Fechter*.

They sent their sons there so as to acquaint them with Italianate ways. Inevitably such young men came to know of the new rapier play in the schools of Venice and Bologna, Padua and Rome. Not only was rapier play Italianate, and therefore something in the fashion, but it was seen to be a more effective form of personal combat than the sword and buckler play they had known at home. What more natural than that they should return home full of the new fashion, anxious to continue their practice in it, determined to introduce it to their friends? Equally naturally, they were followed back to England by Italian teachers of the new rapier play.

But the English are not quite human. Instead of welcoming this new and effective innovation, the English teachers opposed it strongly. More than that, the English sword and buckler man who was not a Master of Defence opposed it. Behind the opposition lay English insularity and xenophobia – perhaps not a hatred of, but certainly a great suspicion of anything non-

A section of the field at Agincourt, illustrating a range of early fifteenth-century weapons. The use of the sword of the period by mounted men is shown very clearly. Their method of engagement differs from that in use against infantry where it was more usual to bring the opponent alongside before delivering a thrust or a cut downwards at head or shoulder. The devastating effect of the lance used by the mounted knight is shown by the impaled figure of the horseman in the right foreground whose body armour has been penetrated by a lance head. Archers are shown harassing the opposing horsemen and a pikeman stands ready in the left foreground to impale the horse of any charging knight. From a manuscript in the possession of the Lambeth Palace Library, London.

English. The attitude, which still persists, arises more out of a sense of national insecurity when faced with outside innovation than with a national arrogance. Certainly it is summarised admirably in that most English of works on weapon play, George Silver's *Paradoxes of Defence*, which first appeared in 1599.

Silver, describing himself as 'Gentleman', makes his point as early as his sub-title to the work: 'Wherein is proved the true grounds of Fight to be in the short auncient weapons, and that the short Sword hath aduantage of the long Sword or long Rapier. And the weakenesse and imperfection of the Rapier-fights displayed. Together with an Admonition to the noble, ancient, victorious, valiant, and most braue nation of Englishmen, to beware of false teachers of Defence, and how they forsake their owne naturall fights: with a briefe commendation of the noble science or exercising of Armes.' His work is a broadside against rapier play in general, Italian rapier play in particular, and most particularly

against the system published in 1595 by Vincentio Saviolo.

Saviolo had reached England from Padua in 1590. He was an established master of fence, thoroughly schooled in Italian rapier play and well acquainted with the theories and practice of Carança and Narvaez in Spain. He joined Jeronimo, son – apparently – of an earlier Italian teacher in London, Rocco Bonetti, in Jeronimo's school of fence in London. He was an eclectic, teaching what seemed to him the best aspects of both Italian and Spanish play. His insistence on calmness and coolness he seems to have drawn from the Spanish play: 'As soon as your rapier is drawne, put yourselfe presentlye on guard, seeking the advantage, and goe not leaping. . . .' He teaches a circular movement in the fight, with attacks made by 'passing', yet he does not involve himself in the metaphysics and geometry of the Spanish style. His cuts are classified after Marozzo, and his belief in the superiority of the point over the edge is in the tradition of the later Italian masters: 'I would not advise any friend of mine, if he were to fighte for his credite and life, to strike neither riversi, nor mandrittaes, because he puts himselfe in danger of his life: for to use the poynt is much more redye and spends not the like time.'

He defines three types of thrust. The *imbroccata* strikes the opponent over his sword-hand or dagger-hand. The *stoccata* strikes him below his sword-hand or dagger-hand. The *punta riversa* is delivered from the left – the inside line of Grassi. These are if possible to be made on the face or the 'bellye'. Certainly a thrust in either of these areas would be debilitating, but perhaps Saviolo was still aware of the possibility of an opponent wearing a mail shirt under his doublet.

In Saviolo's teaching of his hypothetical pupil Luke, he gives a clear idea of what the *ideal* rapier and dagger fight of the period might have looked like:

'I will now shewe you how to put yourselfe en garde with your Rapier

1 A thrust with the rapier accompanied by a displacement of the body to avoid a counter-thrust.

2 A cut to the wrist with the rapier resulting in a disarm. The victor holds his scabbard and hanger in his left hand for defensive use in place of a dagger. From Sutor's *Künstliches Fechtbuch*.

3 Rapier and dagger fighting.

4 The fight with the single rapier according to Meyer. From *Gründliche Beschreibung*.

and Dagger, for if I desire to make a good scholler, I would myself put his Rapier in one hand and his Dagger in the other, and so place his body in the same sorte, that I have before spoken of in the single Rapier, setting his right foote formost with the pointe of his Rapier drawne in short, and the Dagger helde out at length, bending a little his right knee, with the heel of his right foote directlye against the midst of the lefte, causing him to go round toward the lefte side of his adversarye in a good measure, that he may take his advantage; and then I would thrust a stoccata to his bellye beneath his Dagger, removing my right foote a little towards his lefte side.'

1

Luke is naturally curious to know how he is to react to a thrust coming upwards towards his 'bellye' under his left hand.
Vincentio replies:

'The scholler must break it downward with the pointe of his Dagger toward his lefte side, and then put a stoccata to my bellye beneath my Dagger, in which time I, breaking it with the pointe of my Dagger, goe a little aside towards his lefte hand and make an imbroccata above his Dagger; and the scholler shall breake the imbroccata with his Dagger upward, parting circularely with his right foote toward my lefte side, and so thrust unto mee an imbroccata above my Dagger, in which time, with the pointe of my Dagger, I will beate it outward toward my lefte side and answere him with a stoccata in the bellye under his Dagger, parting circularely with my right foote toward his lefte side, stepping toward my lefte side with his right foote; at which time I must moove with my bodye to save my face, and breake his pointe toward my right side, answering him with a riversa to the head, and so retire with my right foote. At this time he must go forward with his lefte foote in the place of my right, and his Dagger high and straite, turning his sword hand so that his pointe may go directlye to my bellye, and he must take the riversa on his swoorde and Dagger.'

2

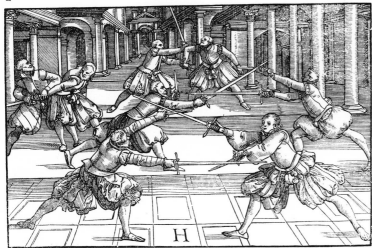

3

4

The impression is of coolness and calculation, of skill produced by long and laborious practice. Yet Silver will have none of it. Against Saviolo's picture of the *ideal* fight with rapier and dagger, he sets the *real* fight as it in fact took place outside the fencing school. Of the death of Jeronimo, Saviolo's partner, he says:

'*Jeronimo* this gallant was valiant, and would fight indeed, and did, as you shall heare. He being in a Coch with a wench that he loved well, there was one *Cheese*, a very tall man, in his fight naturall English, for he fought with his Sword and Dagger, and in Rapier-fight had no skill at all. This *Cheese* having a quarrell to *Jeronimo*, overtooke him upon the way, himselfe being on horsebacke, did call to *Jeronimo*, and bad him come forth of the Coch or he would fetch him, for he was come to fight with him. *Jeronimo* presently went forth of the Coch and drew his Rapier and dagger, put himself into his best ward or *Stoccata* which ward was taught by himselfe and *Vincentio*, and by them best allowed of, to be the best ward to stand upon in fight for life, either to assault the enemie, or stand and watch his comming, which ward it should seeme he ventured his life upon, but howsoever with all the fine Italienated skill *Jeronimo* had, *Cheese* with his Sword with two thrustes ran into the bodie and slue him.'

And of Rocco Bonetti, whom Jeronimo succeeded as head of the Italian school of fence in London, Silver says, 'At Queene Hith he drew his Rapier upon a waterman, where he was thoroughly beaten with Oares and Stretchers. . . .'

But it was foreign influence in English swordplay that Silver was really opposed to, rather than just the play with rapier and dagger, for even the two-handed sword in the hands of an Italian cannot prevail against the sword and buckler in the hands of a 'tall' Englishman:

'There was one *Austen Bagger*, a verie tall gentleman of his handes, not

1 Aspects of German personal combat in the later
sixteenth century. From Meyer's *Gründliche
Beschreibung.*

2 Sword with Saxon hilt and Spanish blade, c. 1570.
Victoria and Albert Museum.

The English quarterstaff man facing Spanish rapiers
and daggers. Both the picture and the caption above
it are in the tradition of George Silver's *Paradoxes
of Defence.*

1

2

standing much upon his skill, but carying the
valiant hart of an Englishman, upon a time being
merrie amongst his friendes, said he would go
fight with *Signior Rocco,* presently went to
Signior Rocco his house in the *Blackfriers,* and
called to him in this maner: *Signior Rocco,* thou
that art thought to be the onely cunning man in the
world with thy weapon, thou that takest upon
thee to hit anie Englishman with a thrust upon
anie button, thou that takest upon thee to come
over the seas, to teach the valiant Noblemen and
Gentlemen of *England* to fight, thou cowardly
fellow come out of thy house if thou dare for thy
life, I am come to fight with thee. *Signior Rocco*
looking out at a window, perceiving him in the
street to stand readie with his Sword and Buckler,
with his two hand Sword drawne, with all speed
ran into the street, and manfully let flie at *Austen
Bagger,* who most bravely defended himselfe,
and presently closed with him, and stroke up his
heeles, and cut him over the breech, and trode
upon him, and most grievously hurt him under
his feet; yet in the end *Austen* of his good nature
gave him his life, and there left him.'

So much, Silver says, for 'Schoole-trickes and
jugling gambalds.' 'Bring me to a Fencer, I will
bring him out of his fence trickes with good
downe right blowes, I will make him forget his
fence trickes I will warrant him.'

In another account of *real* rapier play, as
opposed to the ideal picture that emerges from the
texts of the Masters, Silver describes what must
have been a common enough occurrence:

'Two Captaines at
Southampton even as they were going to take
shipping upon the key, fel at strife, drew their
Rapiers, and presently, being desperate, hardie
or resolute, as they call it, with all force and over
great speed, ran with their rapiers one at the
other, & were both slaine.'

In contrast with the nice points of honour concerning the way in which one man might invite

Three to One.

Being, An Englifh Spanifh Combat,
Performed by a Wefterne Gentleman, of Tauyftoke in Deuonfhire,
with an Englifh Quarter Staffe, againft Three Spanifh
Rapiers and Poniards, at Sherries in Spaine,
The fifteene day of Nouember, 1625.
In the prefence of Dukes, Condes, Marquiffes, and other Great
Dons of Spaine, being the Counfell of Warre.
The Author of this Booke, and Actor in this Encounter, R. Peecke.

Printed at London for I.T. and are to be fold at his Shoppe.

**Saxon sword from the third quarter of the
sixteenth century. Victoria and Albert Museum.**

another to fight with him, Silver gives a clear idea
of what must actually have happened in many
cases:

'This *Vincentio* proved
himself a stout man not long before he died. . . .
Upon a time at *Wels* in Somersetshire, as he was
in great braverie amonst manie gentlemen of
good accompt, with great boldnesse he gave out
speeches, that he had bene thus manie yeares in
England, and since that the time of his first
comming, there was not yet one Englishman, that
could once touch him at the single Rapier, or
Rapier and Dagger. A valiant gentleman being
there amongst the rest, his English hart did rise
to heare this proude boaster, secretly sent a
messenger to one *Bartholomew Bramble* a friend
of his, a verie tall man both of his hands and
person, who kept a schoole of Defence in the
towne, the messenger by the way made the
maister of Defence acquainted with the mind of
the gentleman that sent for him, and of all what
Vincentio had said, this maister of Defence presently came. . . . Then said the maister of Defence: Sir I have a schoole of Defence in the
towne, will it please you to go thither. Thy
schoole, said maister *Vincentio*? what shall I do
at thy schoole? play with me (said the maister)
at the Rapier and Dagger, if it please you. Play
with thee said maister *Vincentio*? if I play with
thee I will hit thee 1. 2. 3. 4. thrustes in the eie
together. Then said the maister of Defence, if
you can do so, it is the better for you, and the
worse for me, but surely I can hardly beleeve that
you can hit me: but yet once againe I hartily
pray you good Sir, that you will go to my schoole,
and play with me. Play with thee said maister
Vincentio (verie scornefully?) by God me scorne
to play with thee. With that word scorne, the
maister of Defence was verie much moved, and
up with his great English fist, and stroke maister
Vincentio such a boxe on the eare that he fell over
and over, his legges just against a Butterie hatch,
whereon stood a great blacke Jacke: the maister of
Defence fearing the worst, against *Vincentio* his

rising, catcht the blacke Jacke into his hand, being more than halfe full of Beere. *Vincentio* lustily start up, laying his hand upon his Dagger, and with the other hand pointed with his finger, saying, very well: I will cause to lie in the Gaile for this geare, 1. 2. 3. 4. yeares. And well said the maister of Defence, since you will drinke no wine, will you pledge me in Beere? I drinke to all the cowardly knaves in *England*, and I thinke thee to be the veriest coward of them all: with that he cast all the Beere upon him: notwithstanding *Vincentio* having nothing but his guilt Rapier, and Dagger about him, and the other for his defence the blacke Jacke, would not at that time fight it out. . . .'

Silver is by no means simply destructive, although his only comment on Vincentio Saviolo's book is, 'I have read it over'. He puts forward a well-developed system of his own in which he mentions 'the perfect length' of weapons, and deals not only with the sword and buckler, but also with the two-handed sword, the 'Battel-axe' and a wide range of polearms. The worst weapon, 'an imperfect and insufficient weapon, and not worth the speaking of; but now being highly esteemed, therefore not to be left un-remembred; that is, the single Rapier, and Rapier and Poiniard.' And the best – in single combat, though perhaps not in the crush of pitched battle – 'The Welch hooke or Forrest bill, hath advantage against all maner of weapons whatsoever.'

He is out of tune with almost everyone in his attitude to the use of the point:

'I have knowne a Gentleman hurt in Rapier fight, in nine or ten places through the bodie, armes, and legges, and yet hath continued in his fight, & afterward hath slaine the other, and come home and hath bene cured of all his wounds without maime, & is yet living. But the blow being strongly made, taketh somtimes cleane away the hand from the arme, hath manie times bene seene. Againe, a full blow upon the head or face with a short sharpe Sword, is most commonly death. A full blow upon the necke, shoulder, arme, or legge, indangereth life, cutteth off the veines, muscles, and sinewes, perisheth the bones: these wounds made by the blow, in respect of perfect healing, are the loss of limmes, or maimes incurable for ever.'

But he does remind us that there are more ways of doing a man to death than skewering him with a rapier, whilst defending oneself with a 'frog picking Poiniard'. And he reminds us too that whilst some Europeans were fighting one another in the manner of Agrippa, Meyer and Saviolo with the rapier, many others fought with pole-arms and battle-axes, Zweyhänder and broad-swords and bucklers.

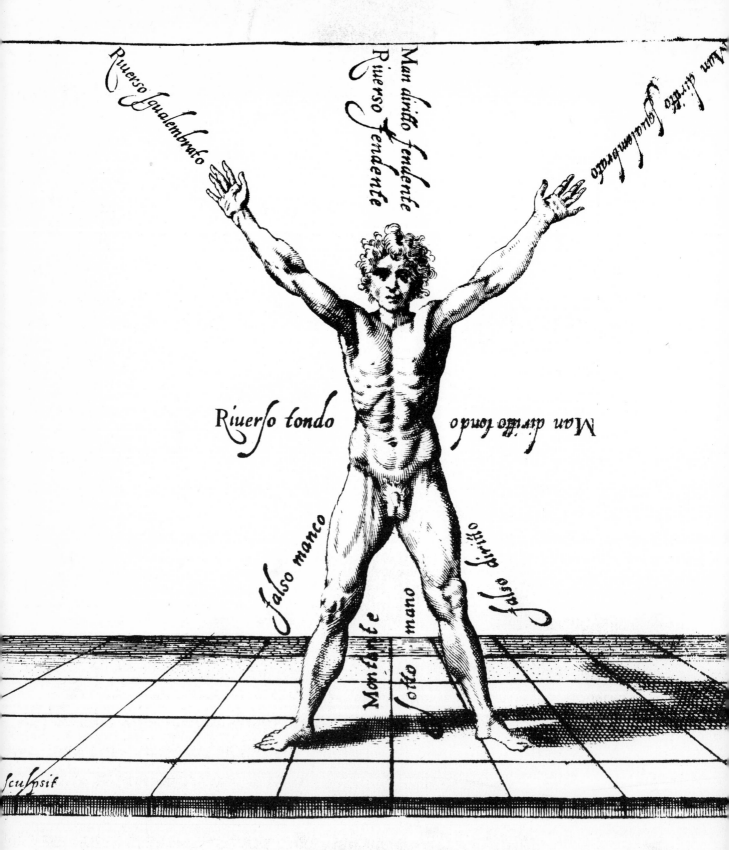

Riuerso Sgualembrato

Man diritto Fendente

Riuerso Fendente

Man diritto Sgualembrato

Riuerso tondo

Man diritto tondo

falso manco

Montante

falso diritto

sculpsit

DISCORSO SOPRA LA PRIMA GVARDIA

formata nel cauare la spada del

Chapter Five

THE SUPREMACY OF THE POINT

Despite the efforts of George Silver in England to halt the spread of rapier play, it was nevertheless the form of personal fighting that triumphed in the seventeenth century. The reason, we must conclude, was a simple one: of all the ways of dispatching an opponent into the next world, the rapier provided the most effective. Even Joseph Swetnam, 'tutor in the skill of weapons' to Prince Henry of England, writing in 1617, makes it quite clear that only the rapier and dagger remained in fashion, although the sword and buckler were still carried by a few obstinate people. 'The Rapier and the close-hilted Dagger' he considers to be 'the finest and most comeliest weapons that ever were used in England. The short sword against the Rapier is little better than a tobacco-pipe.'

Swetnam can hardly be said to have advanced the theory of personal combat in England. In fact, at this time it seems that the English still persisted in rapiers and daggers of disproportionate length which were certainly disappearing elsewhere. Swetnam thinks that a rapier with a blade-length of at least four feet is 'a reasonable length', and recommends a dagger two feet long. It seems surprising that such weapons should have been so superior in use to those that Silver advocated.

But Swetnam gives us some idea of the weapons used for practice in personal combat. Previously, the practice weapon had been the actual weapon of combat with the edges and point 'foiled' – still a formidable piece of equipment, quite capable of putting out an eye or smashing a wrist. Now a weapon specially designed for practice appears. It has a metal button riveted on the end, round which padding and leather are wrapped. The final result is a covering 'the bignesse of a tennis ball'. It was intended to protect the eyes from damage. It is surprising that the face mask had still not been invented, since a smack in the eye with a leather-covered tennis ball delivered 'on the pass' could hardly have improved that organ. We must not think, of course, that the introduction of a special weapon

The target, according to Fabris, showing the principal directions of attack.

Some of the wide variety of body postures recommended by Fabris in rapier play.

A practice rapier and dagger, possibly German, of the early seventeenth century. Victoria and Albert Museum.

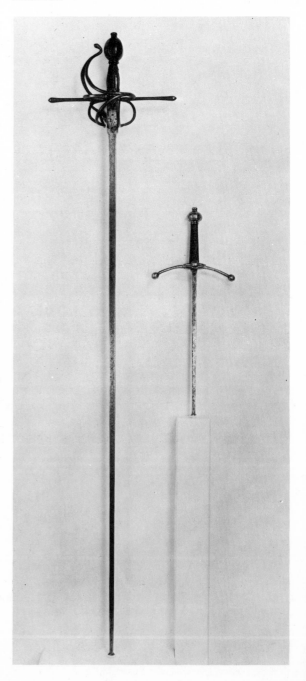

for practice meant that practice was undertaken for its own sake. For more than a hundred and fifty years after Swetnam's time the principal purpose of all fencing practice was to prepare the student for actual combat. And even practice with the 'foiled' weapon was not without its dangers. Godfrey, writing in England a hundred years later, could still say: 'I have purchased my knowledge with many a broken Head and Bruise in every part of me.'

But it is to Italy that we must turn again to see the final perfection of theory and practice relating to the use of the rapier. Three names dominate the early seventeenth century, and set the seal for much of the later play of the next century with the small sword; Salvator Fabris, Nicoletto Giganti and Ridolfo Capo Ferro.

Fabris, born in Bologna in 1544, can be said to crystallise all the best in sixteenth-century theory and practice, and at the same time to contribute new ideas. He carries the authority not only of a sound theorist, but also of a practitioner of wide experience. He had travelled in Germany, France and Spain and must have studied the practice of Meyer, Sainct Didier and Carança. In Italy he must have known at first hand the practice of Agrippa, Viggiani and Grassi – perhaps even of Marozzo himself. During the last ten years of the sixteenth century he taught at the Danish court of Christian IV in Copenhagen, where, in 1606, his book *Sienz E Pratica D'Arme* was published.

Grassi and Viggiani had both suggested that the thrust was a more effective attack than the cut. Fabris insisted on this. To him the cut was very definitely inferior to the use of the point. This was a crucial development since, if it were to be widely accepted, it would mean that the weight of the rapier could be reduced. A blade, to be used for cutting, must be wide enough to take two effective edges. Such width increases its weight considerably. But a blade for use exclusively in thrusting play need only to be wide enough to remain comparatively stiff. Such a reduction in weight leads to a better balance – a certain blade-heaviness is necessary in an

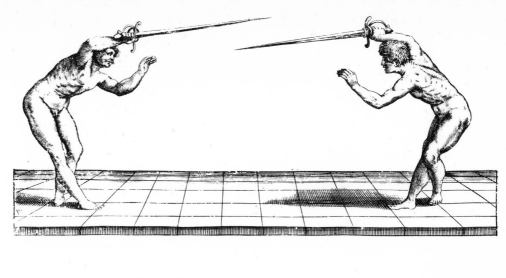

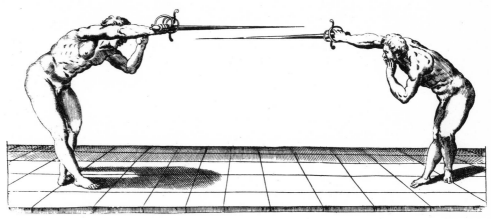

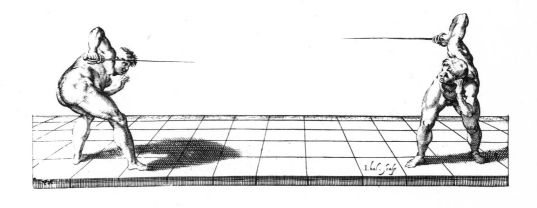

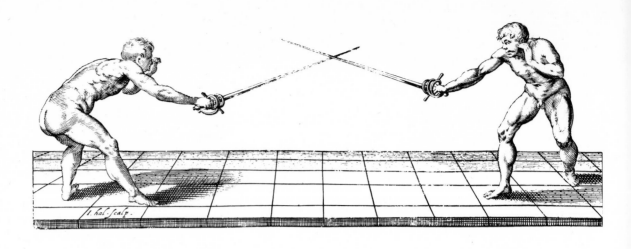

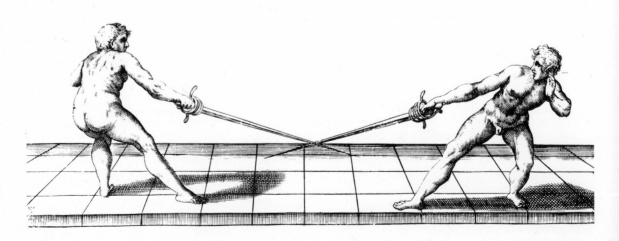

The engagement of blades – the *trovare di spada* – taught by Fabris.

effective cutting weapon – and to much greater mobility. Greater mobility of the rapier leads to its increased use in defence, and ultimately to the discarding of the dagger. And with the discarding of the dagger, a new kind of play is possible.

The play Fabris teaches is supple and flexible. Although he mentions only the four main guards already well established, he advocates an infinite variety of bodily attitudes to be adopted behind the sword-hand. And he recommends the adoption of the *contra postura* – a bodily position similar to that of the opponent. The wider the range of bodily postures a fighter can adopt, the more difficult the job of his adversary. The wide range of attitudes envisaged by Fabris is apparent from the illustrations taken from his work. The guard begins to change its nature with Fabris. Although it is still mainly an attitude from which a movement can be initiated, he suggests that it might also constitute a defence in itself. Sword and body in the *en garde* position should be placed so that one fighter cannot hit the other merely by thrusting straight forward. To do so he must first change the position of his own weapon. Connected with this Fabris mentions a guard position in which the fighters are close enough to hit one another without advancing – the *misura stretta*, the 'close measure'. In such a position the two swords are in contact with one another, and the true guard – that which actually 'guards' part of the target without the fighter having to move at all to avoid an attack – becomes possible.

With the engagement of blades – the *trovare di spada* – a new problem arises. If the guard actually 'guards' part of the target, then the attacker must 'disengage' his blade before he makes his attack. Fabris deals in detail with how this disengagement should be made. He says, in Castle's translation, 'When the enemy tries to engage your sword, or to beat it aside: without letting him engage or beat it, you must make a *cavatione di tempo*' – a disengagement by dropping the point of the sword below the adversary's blade, and lifting it again on the other side. 'A *contra cavatione* is that which can be done, during the time that the enemy disengages, by disengaging yourself, so that he shall find himself situated as before.' Such a statement almost carries us into the duelling moves of the nineteenth century. Despite Fabris' acceptance of the defence by counter-attack, the statement contains the idea of a parry with the sword as a defensive move in its own right. If on one fighter's disengagement his opponent responds with the *contra cavatione*, then the opponent has in effect *parried* in the modern sense. That is, he has used a movement of his sword in order simply to defend himself and not as part of a counter-attack. And it is significant to notice that Fabris' *contra cavatione* is a *circular* movement, since only with such a movement would the enemy 'find himself situated as before'. As we have seen, this is not only a *contra cavatione*, it is also a circular parry, and this is a significant development.

It is not really surprising that the concept of the parry as something separate from the counter-attack, should have taken so long to evolve. The parry had, of course, existed with the buckler, the dagger, the cloak and the mailed left hand, but not with the sword. The defence with the sword had been the counter-attack, the move whereby a fighter, when attacked, launched a counter-attack which not only beat aside or deflected the attacking weapon, but *at the same time* struck the attacker. This was the only defence possible with the sword, as long as it remained ill-balanced and heavy. If Fabris' comments on the disengagement indicate nothing else, they certainly show how much the rapier had developed since the days of Agrippa. But there is a further point that is significant. As we have seen, in describing the *contra cavatione*, he describes in effect a new kind of parry. The circular movement of the sword-point as a means of defence is not new. It was taught by many earlier masters as a form of universal parry, valuable in a *mêlée* or in a confined space. What is new is the idea that it might be incorporated into the fight itself as a new form of parry.

The fight with the single rapier according to Fabris.
The great flexibility of the fighting style is apparent
and the wide range of body positions.

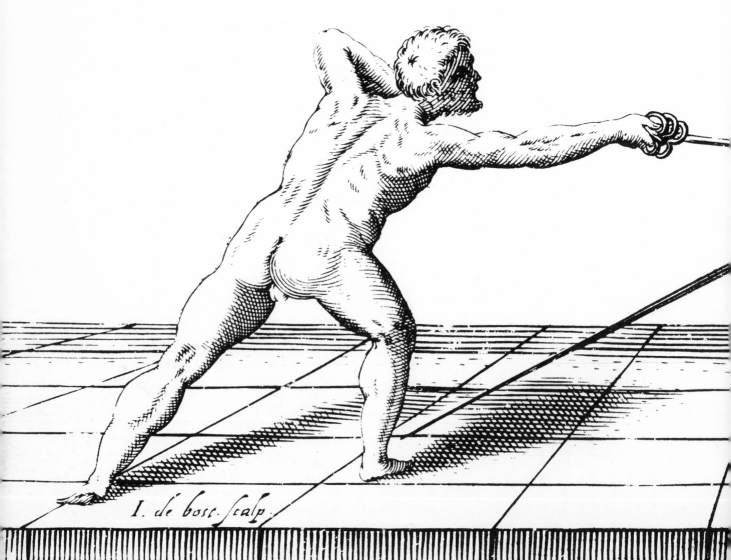

I. de bosc. scalp.

All hits are made by the counter-thrusts rather than
by ripostes following parries. It is interesting to note
that the left hand is not used to deflect the
opponent's blade.

The use of the left hand in Fabris' system. The hand deflects the opponent's blade and at the same time a counter-thrust is delivered with the sword.

He deals with the practical problems of combat and the way in which his teaching can be applied to them. He is concerned, for example, not only with rapier opposed to rapier, but with dagger opposed to sword, cloak against sword and dagger, sword opposed to pike or halberd. He mentions, as Silver had done before him, the use of the pommel as a knuckle-duster in close combat, and he is as concerned as the Italian masters before him with the various ways in which an opponent might be disarmed. Castle says of him:

'The science of arms owes to Fabris the elucidation of many hitherto half-understood principles: a clear definition of the word "guard", in the name of "contra guardia"; of opposition, which he calls "trovare di spada"; of disengagement; circular parries and their deceptions, which he calls "contra cavatione" and "ricavatione" respectively; of the nature of feints; of time, and of distance.

'Had Fabris taught his pupils the lunge . . . nothing would have been wanting in his method to make it as perfect a system of fence as could be devised for the rapier.'

But despite the work of Agrippa, which at least suggested the 'lunge', Fabris did not invent that vital movement. The first fully worked out description of the movement, and of the essential recovery from it, belongs to Giganti.

Giganti describes the lunge – the method of delivering the point by the shortest and fastest means – and the recovery from it, in these terms (Castle's translation):

'To deliver the stoccata lunga, place thyself in a firm attitude, rather collected than otherwise, so as to be capable of further extension. Being thus on guard, extend thy arm and advance the body at the same time, and bend the right knee as much as possible, so that thy opponent may be hit before he can parry. Wert thou to advance the whole body, thy adversary would perceive it, and, by taking a time,

parry and strike thee at the same moment. . . .

'In order to retire, begin the movement with the head, and the body will naturally follow on; then likewise draw back thy foot; if thou wert to retire it first, both head and body would remain in danger. . . .'

Giganti's view of how one might best kill a man with a rapier and yet remain free from injury oneself is 'wonderfully perfect and complete in comparison with the mass of those which were written before it'. Two guards – quarte and tierce – are sufficient for him. The blades of the opposing swords are 'engaged' – and the two guards do actually 'guard' the target, in the sense that if one fighter simply extends his arm and executes Giganti's *stoccata lunga* he will not hit his opponent. To do so, he must first 'disengage' – that is, drop the point of his weapon below his opponent's blade, and lift it on the other side before lunging. His approach is simple and practical: behind it one senses his awareness of the end-product of any system of fence of this time – actual combat.

But the peak of achievement of the Italian tradition is reached with the work of Capo Ferro. It is at the same time the peak of rapier play. Capo Ferro fixes permanently the principles on which all later sword-play is based, at least in those weapons in which the point predominates. As Silver had done before him, he defines the proper length of a sword. It should be, he says, twice as long as the arm. In the average man, this would perhaps give an overall length of four feet and a blade-length of some thirty-nine inches – a considerable improvement on Swetnam's idea of some years later, that a blade-length of at least forty-eight inches was necessary for the rapier.

Not only is he very much in favour of the thrust, he regards the cut as having very little place in rapier fighting, being really more suitable for use on horseback in conjunction with the broadsword. His reason is, of course, a purely practical one – the cut takes longer to deliver than the thrust, and requires the attacker to move closer to his opponent in order to deliver it – a

The wide range of guard positions recommended by Fabris for use in the rapier and dagger fight. Not only do the positions of the weapons themselves vary, but there is considerable variation in the positions of the body itself.

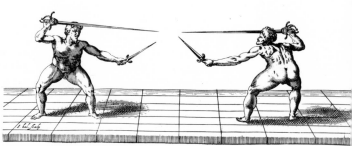

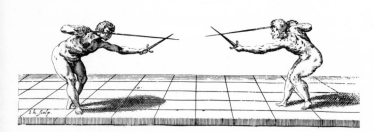

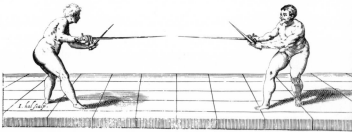

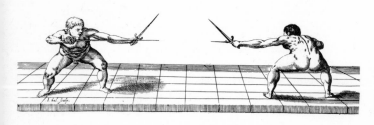

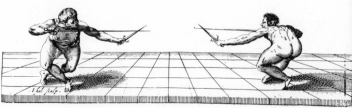

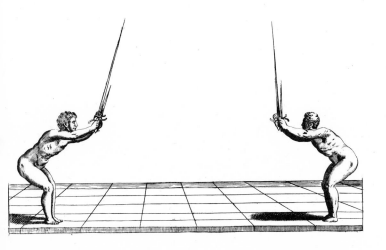

fact which increases the danger of a counter-thrust.

In the guard position, as the illustrations make clear, the right foot is advanced. To close the distance between one fighter and the other, and so come close enough to deliver a thrust, the attacker 'advances' by stepping forward with the right foot first and then bringing the left foot up towards it. From such a position Giganti's *stoccata lunga* can be launched. And in the recovery from the lunge, the left arm is to be used as a counter-weight to help the fighter to return to the guard position more quickly.

Despite this, Capo Ferro had no objection to the use of the dagger or cloak in the left hand, as is clear from his illustrations as well as those of Alfieri which seem so closely based on them. But these were no longer necessary as the *sole* means of defence. They were used in conjunction with the rapier and also to facilitate its use in attack. In theory it was becoming increasingly unnecessary to employ the left hand in defence, although in combat a man naturally used all the tools that were available to him.

With Capo Ferro and his fellow Italians of the period a new shape for the rapier fight emerges. Earlier works had recommended a fight that was circular, a fight where the combatants moved round one another, seeking an opening, a fight in which an attacking or a defensive move was made by a step to one side or the other. But with Capo Ferro we see the establishment of the fight up and down a straight line – a fight shape entirely contrary to the shape laid down by Carança and Narvaez, with their magic circle. Capo Ferro was well aware of this, and gives advice on how to manage an opponent of the Spanish school.

No doubt under pressure from those who found themselves engaged from time to time in un-provoked combat, Capo Ferro mentions as a general parry, of use in a confined space or against more than one opponent, a semi-circular move-ment of the blade describing an arc with the point from the level of the opponent's left shoulder to the level of his left knee, passing through his right

The fight with rapier and dagger according to
Fabris, showing the great flexibility of body movement and the method of parrying with the dagger
and counter-thrusting with the rapier (pages 78–81).

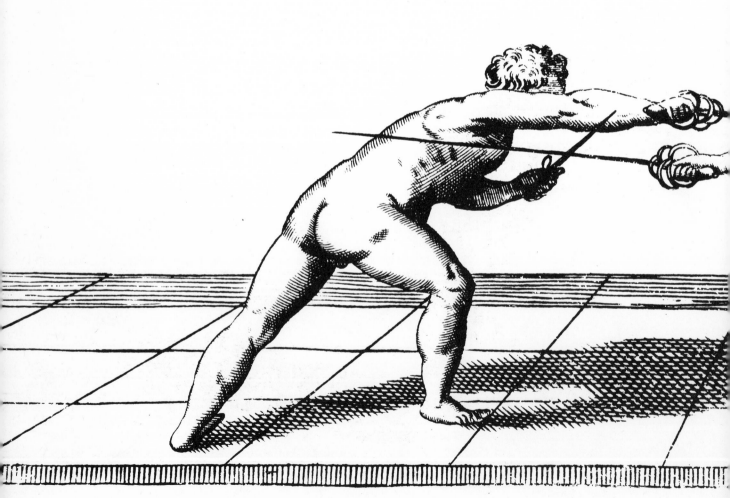

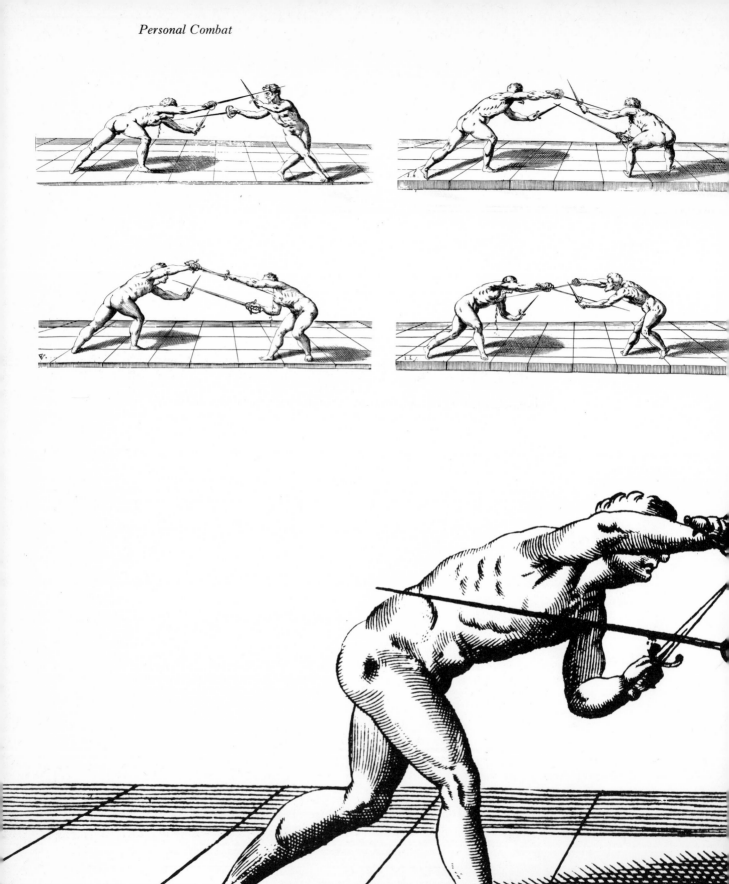

Fabris' guard positions for use in the rapier and cloak fight. The idea of adopting a posture similar to that taken up by the opponent is particularly clear here.

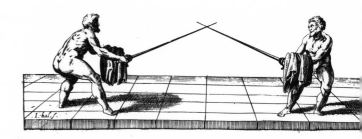

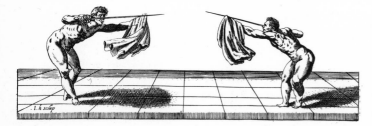

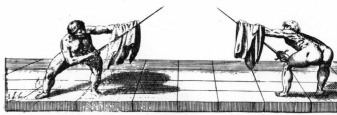

The rapier and cloak combination in action. As the illustrations make clear, the principal use of the cloak is to deflect the opponent's blade and create an opening for a counter-attack.

The cloak could also be used to envelop the whole
of the opposing sword and sword-arm, or it could
be flung into the opponent's face.

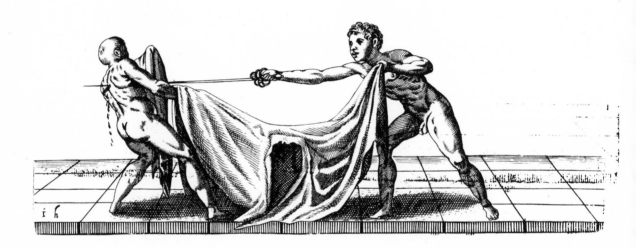

1 The butt stroke with the rapier guard.

2 Seizure of the opponent's guard and a counter-thrust.

3 The disarm by seizure of the opponent's guard.

4 Chop to the throat on the opponent's attack accompanied by a counter-thrust with the rapier.

5 The single rapier opposed to the pike.

6 The hit with both rapier and dagger.

2

4

6

hip. Such a movement does cover all the vital points of the target – which by Capo Ferro's time included the chest just as much as the face and belly – and would offer as much protection as could be expected against a surprise attack by three or four cut-throats in some narrow Florentine street in the Italy of the early seventeenth century.

We can build a picture of the ideal rapier fight from Capo Ferro's own notes:

'The fighters come on guard in terza – a low guard covering the "outside line" – the rapier held out horizontally, with the point menacing the opponent's body. Neither makes any complex moves such as might expose him to a counter-thrust. Each watches the other's sword hand as being the best way of anticipating what he is going to do. When they have summed one another up, one makes a simple feint in the hope of persuading his opponent to uncover himself. His opponent responds with a circular parry followed at the same time with a thrust made by 'passing' – stepping forward with the left foot to shorten the distance between the fighters. Neither fighter parries without at the same time thrusting. Even when a parry is made with the dagger or the cloak, it is accompanied at the same time with a thrust with the rapier. When one fighter forgets momentarily to threaten his opponent with his point, his sword wrist is attacked with a thrust. Disengagements are met with counter-disengagements and thrusts at the most convenient part of the body. Those attacks which are not delivered "on the pass" are delivered with a lunge, the recovery from which is helped by movement of the left hand. If one fighter is unduly aggressive, his attacks will be met at once by a counter-attack; alternatively, the defender will step backwards to avoid the attack, and at once counter with a thrust. Equally, the aggressor's sword wrist can be attacked with a cut as it advances. Individual moves are fast, once a fighter has decided on them. But that decision is not made lightly, since both fighters are well aware of the outcome of failure. The fighters no longer move in a circle round one another, but back and forwards along an imaginary straight line.'

The first quarter of the seventeenth century, then, saw the fight with the rapier reach perfection under the leadership of the Italians. The length and weight of the weapon had been substantially reduced, the cut had almost disappeared in favour of the thrust, the defence with the dagger, cloak or buckler in the left hand was disappearing in favour of defence with the sword itself.

1   **Guard position with the rapier and dagger according to Capo Ferro.**

2   **The engagement of blades with the single rapier.**

3   **The lunge – the *botta lunga* – with the single rapier.**

3

The fight with the single rapier, according to Capo
Ferro. The fight takes place up and down an
imaginary straight line, rather than in the circular
pattern characteristic of earlier rapier play. The
lunge is fully developed. The left hand, however, is
still used, not only to deflect the opposing blade but
also to seize the opponent's sword at the guard.

D   C

The fight with the single rapier, according to Capo
Ferro (*continued*).

A guard recommended by Capo Ferro for the rapier and dagger fight.

The rapier and dagger fight according to Capo Ferro.
The positions of the body are more upright and less
complex than those advocated by Fabris. The
dagger is used defensively to parry an attack, as
well as to initiate one by pushing aside the opposing
blade and so creating an opening for the sword.

1 The rapier and dagger fight according to Capo
Ferro. The dagger can also be used as an attacking
weapon in its own right.

2 The guard for the fight with rapier and cloak.

3 The parry with the cloak accompanied by a
counter-thrust with the rapier.

2

3

Rapier and buckler fighting. The method of securing
the large buckler by a hand-and-arm-grip can be
clearly seen.

1–3 Rapier fighting, according to Alfieri, showing the lunge, opposition with the left hand and the use of the 'displacement' to avoid an attacking sword.

4 The disarm and counter-thrust in single rapier play.

5 The double-hit with rapier and dagger.

6 The counter-thrust with the rapier, accompanying the parry with the cloak.

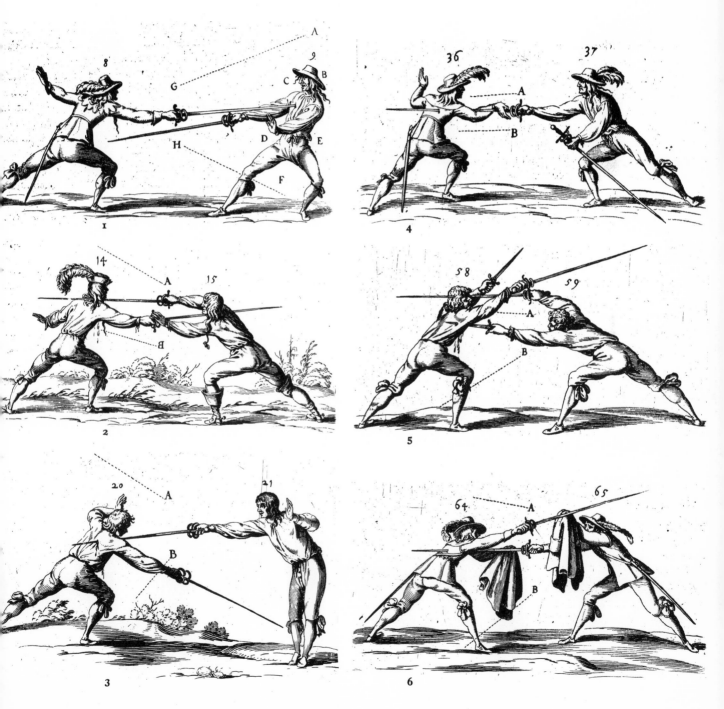

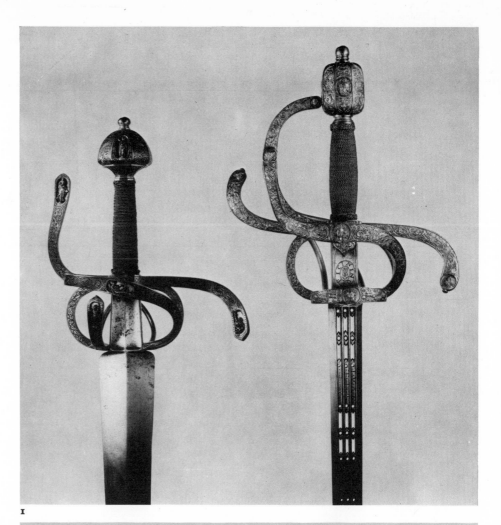

1

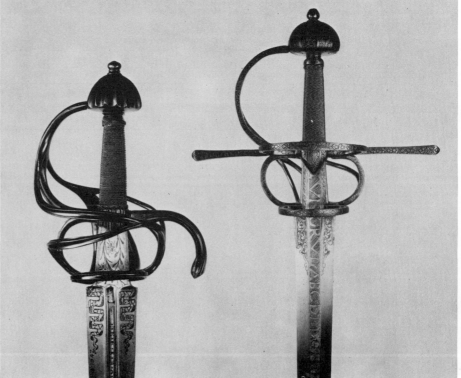

2

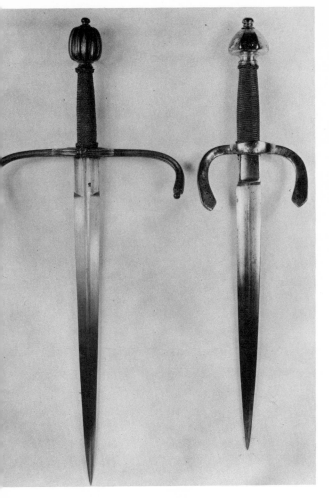

4

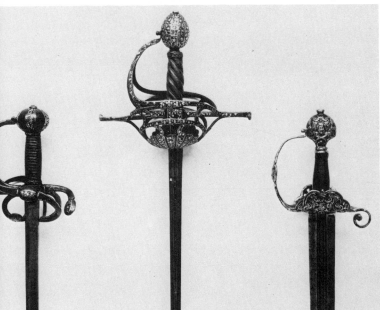

1 & Saxon rapiers of the late sixteenth century.
2   Victoria and Albert Museum.

3   German left-handed daggers of the late sixteenth
century. Victoria and Albert Museum.

4   Saxon daggers c. 1600. Victoria and Albert Museum.

5   Left: English sword of the late sixteenth century.
Centre: rapier with Spanish blade and English hilt
of the early seventeenth century. Right: early
seventeenth-century broadsword. Victoria and
Albert Museum.

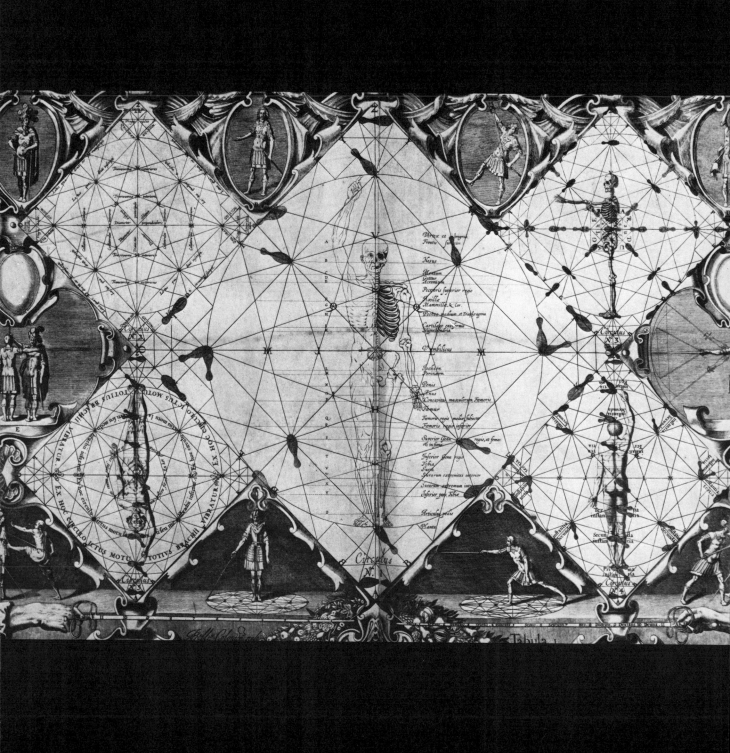

Chapter Six

TRANSITION

National and personal interests affect the development of personal combat as much as they affect human development in other fields. Despite the logic and lucidity of Italian theories, uncluttered as they were with philosophy and mystery, they were not universally accepted. The influence of the Spanish school was considerable and the Spanish style of combat was a fashion much imitated by European 'gentlemen'. The French were particularly influenced by Spanish methods, and a Hispano-French style was evolved. Silver had said of the Spanish style at the end of the sixteenth century:

'The *Spaniard* is now thought to be a better man with his Rapier then is the Italian, Frenchman, high Almaine, or anie other countrie man whatsoever, because they in their Rapier-fight stand upon so manie trickes, that in all the course of a mans life it shall be hard to learne them, and if they misse in doing the least of them in their fight, they are in danger of death. But the *Spaniard* in his fight, both safely to defend himselfe, and to endanger his enemie, hath but one onely lying [general position of the body], and two wards [sword positions] to learne, wherein a man with small practise in a verie short time may become perfect.'

The ideas of Carança and Narvaez do not seem to bear out Silver's views of Spanish 'simplicity'. But we must remember that Silver was first and foremost an opponent of the Italian method. Anything that he could say in favour of the Spanish would naturally detract from the Italian.

Yet Silver's description of the Spanish method is very similar to that given in the work of Girard Thibault:

'This is the maner of the Spanish fight, they stand as brave as they can with their bodies straight upright, narrow spaced, with their feet continually moving, as if they were in a dance, holding forth their armes and Rapiers verie straight against the face or bodies of their enemies:

The complex geometry of the Spanish system of fence.

1 *Below and previous page*
   **The fencing school as visualised by Thibault. The
   geometric patterns on the floor are for the practice
   of accurate foot movements.**

2 **Spanish play with the single rapier according to
   Thibault. The geometric nature of the Spanish
   style, which is apparent in the illustrations, gives the
   play something of the quality of a dance (pages
   111–116).**

& this is the only lying to accomplish that kind of
fight. And this note, that as long as any man shall
lie in that maner with his arme, and point of his
Rapier straight, it shall be impossible for his
adversarie to hurt him, because in that straight
holding forth of his arme, which way soever a
blow shall be made against him, by reason that
his Rapier hilt lyeth so farre before him, he hath
but a verie litle way to move, to make his ward
perfect, in this maner. If a blow be made at the
right side of the head, a verie litle moving of the
hand with the knuckles upward defendeth that
side of the head or bodie, and the point being still
out straight, greatly endangereth the striker: and
so likewise, if a blow be made at the left side of
the head, a verie small turning of the wrist with
the knuckles downward, defendeth that side of
the head and bodie, and the point of the Rapier
much indangereth the hand, arme, face or bodie
of the striker: and if anie thrust be made, the
ward, by reason of the indirections in moving the
feet in maner of dauncing, as aforesaid, maketh
a perfect ward, and still with all the point greatly
endangereth the other. And thus is the Spanish
fight perfect: so long as you can keepe that order,

1

and soone learned, and therefore to be accounted the best fight with the Rapier of all other.'

Thibault was a Frenchman teaching in the Low Countries. His book, published in 1628, is perhaps the most lavish and magnificent in the entire history of literature dealing with the ways of killing a man, yet it is curious to see how little he seems to have been affected by Italian theories. The very title of his work suggests a complexity that seems to contradict Silver's statement: 'Academie de l'Espée, où se demonstrent par Reigles Mathématiques, sur le fondement d'un Cercle Mystèrieux, La Théorie et Pratique des vrais et Jusqu'à present incognus secrets du maniement Des Armes, à pied et à Cheval.' He advocates a single guard position, identical with that described by Silver. The fighters stand facing one another, more sideways-on than square, upright, feet only a little apart, sword and arm extended in a straight line from the shoulder, the points threatening one another's faces. Attacks and defensive moves are made on the 'pass' – moving the feet, as Silver says, 'in maner of dauncing' – and the cut is used as much as the thrust. The fight pattern is still circular, despite Capo Ferro's contention that it is quicker to advance and lunge in a straight line.

The following, in Castle's translation, is Thibault's description of the play of rapiermen in the Spanish style:

'At the same instant that Alexander drops his foot on the point marked G (in the magic circle) Zacharia steps forward and delivers an 'imbrocade' at his breast. The adversaries having previously been on guard at the first instance with their swords held straight and parallel, Alexander began to work round in order to master his "contrary's" blade on the second instance X, on the inner side of the diameter. This doing, at the same moment that he places his right foot on the letter G, and proceeds in a circular manner with the left, Zacharia bears on him, carrying his right foot inside the circle as far as the letter S, on the inner side of the diameter, bending forward on the right foot, and rounding the arm by the same action so as to turn the exterior branch of the sword vertically upwards. Thus he delivers the imbrocade on his adversary's breast, proceeding further by carrying the left foot outside, on the inside of the quadrangle.'

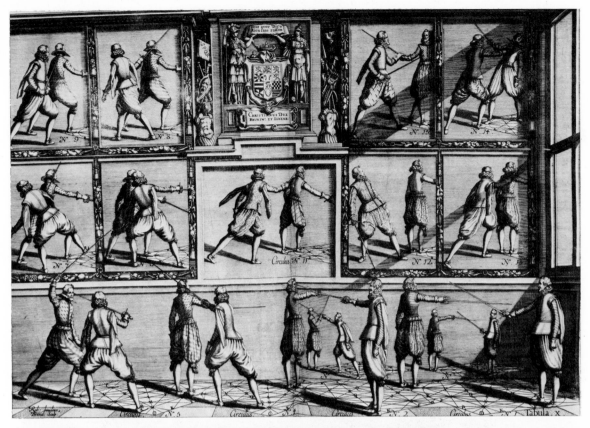

A comparison between these illustrations from
Thibault's book and those from the works of Fabris
and Capo Ferro shows how completely different was
the development of Spanish rapier play from that
of the Italians. The lavish architectural backgrounds
reflect the ritualistic view that the Spanish masters
took of swordplay, a view that today is still
apparent in the bull fight.

If this was the play in which 'a man with small practise in a verie short time may become perfect', then how complex the play of 'the Italian, French-man and high Almaine'!

The Spanish school, whether represented by Spaniards or by such Frenchmen as Thibault, had wide European influence whilst remaining itself unaffected by developments elsewhere. Theory and practice remained substantially as Thibault described it until well into the eighteenth century, and this itself argues considerable merit in the method in actual combat, since it could hardly have lasted if its exponents had not been able to survive combat with opponents from other schools. Even the Spanish weapon, though it became lighter with the passage of time, remained substantially a miniature rapier, with cup-guard, *quillons* and knuckle-bow, for another hundred years. Despite its merits, and particularly the merit of imposing a coolness and lack of passion on fighters, Spanish combat methods remained separate from the mainstream of European developments.

Perhaps the most significant thing about Thibault is that he was French. The Italians had brought personal combat with the rapier to a point beyond which it could hardly be developed further, but it was the French who carried it into the eighteenth century and made the small sword the most lethal non-percussion weapon ever devised. And here it is necessary to look for a moment at the developments in the sword itself, which brought forward the mass of French theories concerning its use.

The Italian masters, as we have seen, insisted on the superiority of the thrust over the cut, but the cut itself was not totally discarded. Even Capo Ferro had recommended a cut at the wrist of an aggressive opponent as being a useful way of stopping his advance. And whilst the cut was still in use, however infrequently, a weapon heavy enough to take an edge was essential. True, there had been one or two swords at the end of the sixteenth century that had all but dispensed with an edge – the excessively long *Verdun* is one

example, the *Flamberg* is another – but they were not typical. The typical weapon, the rapier, had two edges for cutting play, a point and a complexity of guards and counter-guards for the hand. Even in 1628, Thibault recommends that it be some four feet long overall. But the French, by discarding the cut altogether, left the way open for the development of a different kind of weapon, and therefore a different kind of play.

The first development in this direction is the *transition rapier*. A typical example had a knuckle-bow, *pas d'ânes* – the two metal loops below the grip that first began to appear regularly in the early sixteenth century – and a simple sheet-metal guard. The blade in most cases could still take some form of edge, but this was not so much for cutting as to prevent the opponent from executing a disarm by seizing the blade. By the mid-seventeenth century the average blade-length of the weapon was somewhere between thirty and thirty-five inches, by comparison with the blade-length 'of at least four feet' that Swetnam had recommended only thirty years earlier. A comparison of weights indicates the fundamental change that took place as a result of making the sword *exclusively* a thrusting weapon: a weapon such as Swetnam recommended would weigh at least two and a half pounds, whereas the average transition weapon was perhaps a pound lighter. The possibilities of such a transformed weapon were enormous.

Although the rapier and the transition rapier remained the most lethal weapons of personal combat during the first half of the seventeenth century – and certainly the ones to which fighters gave most thought – a variety of cutting weapons coexisted with them. The *Düsack* was still in use in Germany. The broadsword, which was becoming the principal military sword, developed a more complex hilt which evolved by the mid-century into the basket hilt of the horseman. On foot, the 'shearing' sword, with a straight, double-edged blade, and the 'back-sword' with its single-edged and occasionally slightly curved blade, were developments of the earlier broadswords.

Tabula VI.

The single rapier opposed to the rapier and dagger.

Play with these weapons continued to be agile and vigorous, and no fundamental changes in style took place in any way comparable to those which accompanied the development of the thrusting sword.

Increasingly the rapier became identified with the upper classes. This was particularly true in England, where the old cut-and-thrust play of sword and buckler was never totally replaced by the rapier. It seems there was something innate in the northern character that was only satisfied by play with a cutting weapon, where chops could bruise and maim without necessarily proving fatal. When London apprentices settled a quarrel it was not with the rapier, but with the cudgel and buckler that hammered and broke an opponent without piercing his body. The social distinction between rapier and shearing sword is even apparent in Shakespeare. The first stage direction in *Romeo and Juliet* reads, 'Enter Sampson and Gregory, armed with swords and bucklers.' Both these characters are serving-men. Yet when the 'gentlemen' – Romeo, Tybalt, Mercutio, Paris – fight, it is with the rapier. In many ways the distinction between boxing and wrestling is similar. Boxing has always had the support of the upper class – even the rules are those of the Marquess of Queensberry – whilst wrestling, with its vigorous audience-participation, still relies for its support mainly on the 'lower classes'.

It is in the fights of the 'gladiators' – the professional swordsmen of the seventeenth and eighteenth centuries, who conducted the most bloody public bouts with sharp swords, as much to display their prowess as for money – that we see what cutting play was like at its most proficient. Pepys, writing in 1662, describes such a prize-fight:

'. . . walked to the New Theatre, which, since the King's players are gone to the Royal one, is this day begun to be employed by the fencers to play prizes at. And here I come and saw the first prize I ever saw in my life; and it was between one Mathews, who did beat at all

This page and previous page
The Spanish rapier opposing the two-handed sword.

Opposite
Single rapier opposing rapier and buckler.

Following pages
The superiority, in Thibault's view, of the single
rapier even over the musket at point blank range.
The 'coolness' engendered in a swordsman by the
Spanish method, is particularly apparent here.

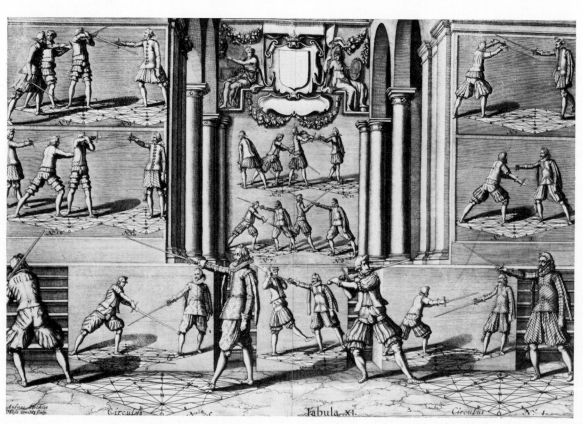

Tabula. VII

TabuLa. XIII

Opposite and following pages
The complicated procedure necessary to load and fire the musket bears out Thibault's confidence in the superiority of the sword over that weapon. From Grose's *Military Antiquities*.

weapons, and one Westwicke, who was soundly cut several times both in the head and legs, that he was all over blood; and other deadly blows they did give and take in very good earnest, till Westwicke was in a sad pickle. They fought at eight weapons, three boutes at each weapon. This being upon a private quarrel, they did it in good earnest; and I felt one of the swords, and found it to be very little, if at all blunter on the edge than the common swords are.'

Pepys gives a very clear idea of a serious combat, since the fighters were both professionals and the motivation was 'a private quarrel'. A contemporary French description (from *An Account of a Journey to the British Isles* by Monsieur Josevin de Rocheford, 1672) of a similar combat is even more bloody. The references to the difference between English and French sword-play of the time are particularly interesting:

'We went to see such a combat, which was performed on a stage in the middle of an amphitheatre, when, on the flourish of trumpets and the beats of drums, the combatants entered, stripped to their shirts. On a signal from the drum, they drew their swords and immediately began to fight, skirmishing a long time without wounds. They were both very skilful and courageous. The tallest had the advantage over the smallest, for, according to the English fashion of fencing, they endeavoured rather to cut than to thrust in the French manner, so that by his height he had the advantage of being able to strike his antagonist on the head, against which the little one was on his guard. He had in his turn one advantage over the tall man in being able to give him the Jarnac stroke, by cutting him on the right ham, which he left in a manner quite unguarded. So that, all things considered, they were equally matched. Nevertheless, the tall one struck the little one on the wrist, which he almost cut off, but this did not prevent him from continuing the fight, after he had been dressed, and taken a glass or two of wine to give him courage,

when he took ample vengeance for his wound; for a little afterwards, making a feint at the ham, the tall man stooping in order to parry it, laid his whole head open, when the little one gave him a stroke which took off a slice of his head and almost all his ear. For my part, I think there is a barbarity and inhumanity in permitting men to kill each other for diversion. The surgeons immediately dressed them and bound up their wounds; which being done, they renewed the combat, and both being sensible of their respective disadvantages, they therefore were a long time without receiving or giving a wound, which was the cause that the little one, failing to parry so exactly, being tired with his long battle, received another stroke on his wounded wrist, which, dividing the sinews, he remained vanquished. . . .'

The superiority of French theory and practice over that of the Italians was established by the work of Besnard in 1653. Besnard had in mind the transition rapier, which still retained some semblance of a cutting edge but which in use could be regarded as exclusively a thrusting weapon. With Besnard we see the beginning of the end of rapier play and its replacement by the play of the small sword which was dominated by French theory and practice during the eighteenth century. With Besnard, although passing is still admitted, the lunge is the main method of attack. We see, too, the establishment of the parry proper, as something separate from the 'time' thrust, in which an attack was met with a counter-attack, which not only beat aside the oncoming blade but hit the opponent at the same time. So the single movement of the counter-attack is replaced by the double movement of parry and riposte. In one move the attacking blade is parried, and in the second a thrust is made through the opening created by the parry. Such a movement was only possible with the much lighter transition weapon.

In defence, the parry with the sword was relied on almost entirely. It was, of course, still possible to dodge and sidestep an attack in actual combat, but in the school of fence this was not encouraged.

March with your rest in your hand.

March, and with your Musket carry your rest.

Unshoulder your Musket.

Poize your Musket

Join your rest to your Musket.

Take forth your Match.

Blow off your Coal.

Cock your Match.

Try your Match.

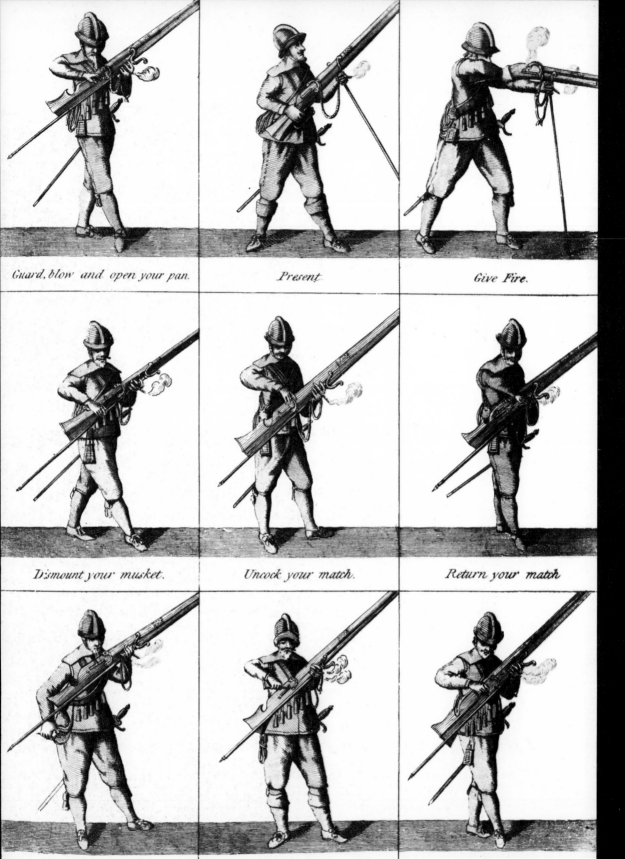

Guard, blow and open your pan.   Present.   Give Fire.

Dismount your musket.   Uncock your match.   Return your match

Clear your pan.   Prime your pan.   Shut your pan.

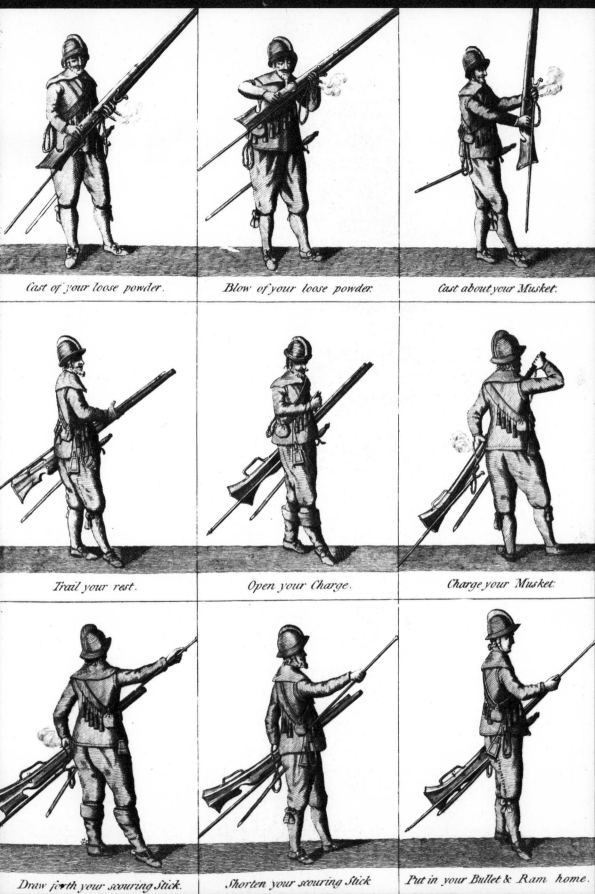

Cast of your loose powder.	*Blow of your loose powder.*	*Cast about your Musket.*
Trail your rest.	*Open your Charge.*	*Charge your Musket.*
Draw forth your scouring Stick.	*Shorten your scouring Stick*	*Put in your Bullet & Ram home.*

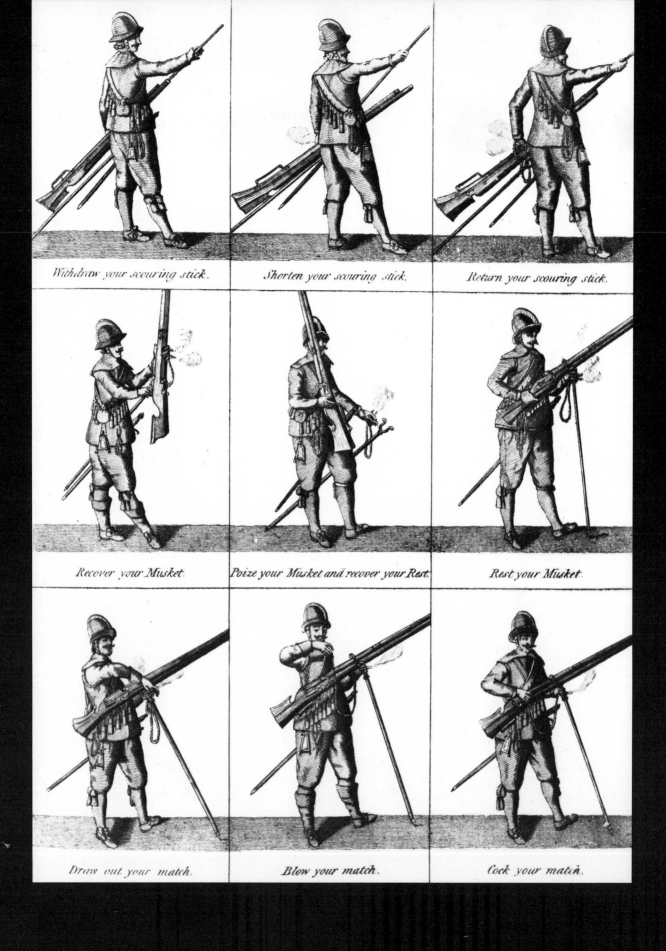

Withdraw your scouring stick.

Shorten your scouring stick.

Return your scouring stick.

Recover your Musket.

Poize your Musket and recover your Rest.

Rest your Musket.

Draw out your match.

Blow your match.

Cock your match.

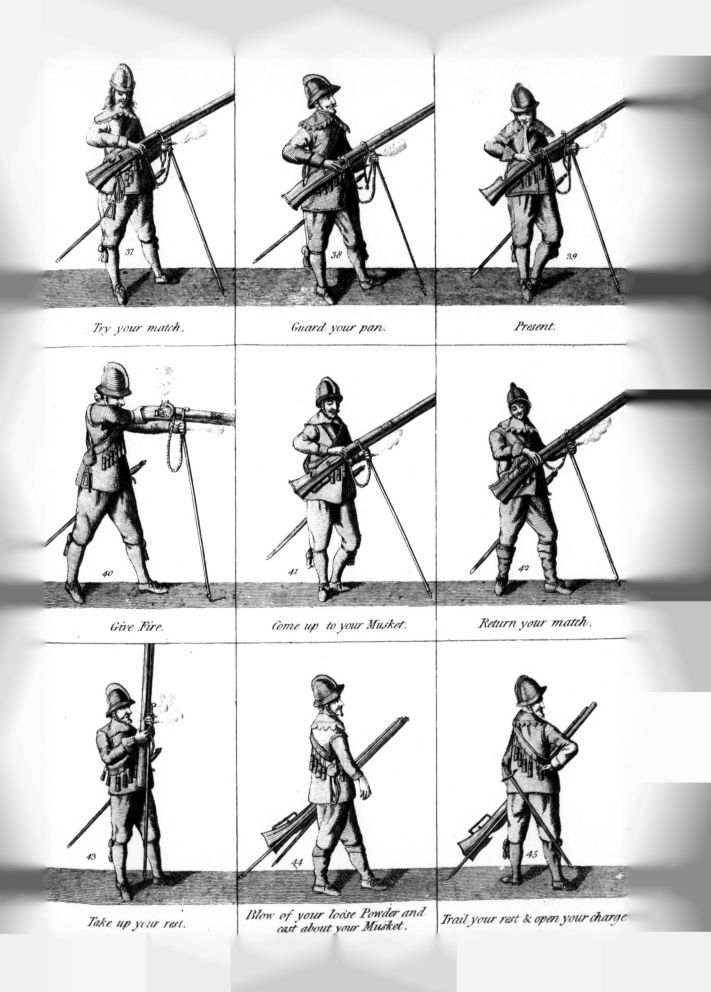

Try your match.

Guard your pan.

Present.

Give Fire.

Come up to your Musket.

Return your match.

Take up your rest.

Blow of your loose Powder and
cast about your Musket.

Trail your rest & open your charge

Bring up your Musket.

Poize your Musket & recover your Rest.

Shoulder your Musket.

Nor was the parry with the left hand. This was no doctrinaire idea; the whole of sword training was still directed to serious combat. But the parry with the left hand was thought to be less effective and less secure than the parry with the sword. Besnard introduced a new quality of *élan* into the gruesome business of taking four inches of steel in the face, by teaching the *révérence* – the series of movements with sword and body which constituted the formal salute to an opponent before a bout, and which in later years became so complex that it required a good deal of practice to memorise and perfect. It was not apparently sufficient to send a man into the next world with expedition, it must also be done with finesse. And lest we lose sight of the serious business that lay behind the theory of this period, the business of killing a man without being killed oneself, there is the *botte du paysan* of La Touche to remind us. This particular *botte* converts the sword into a bayonet. It was executed by gripping one's sword-blade with the left hand and so turning it into a two-handed weapon, beating aside the opponent's blade, stepping into him on the 'pass' and stabbing him in the belly.

It is impossible to say when the transition rapier turned into the small sword. Certainly the way was open for the development when the idea of cutting with the rapier was discarded altogether. But it was established before the last quarter of the seventeenth century, with simple guard, *pas d'ânes* and knuckle-bow and its stiff, triangular or lozenge-section blade. And the names most closely associated with its use in combat are all French – Le Perche, Liancour and Labat.

There is a precision about the works of these three men, characteristic of the French school. Their guards are simple, the parries they recommend are economical and effective. To face any one of them in actual combat must have been a devastating experience. They attack on the lunge and fight up and down an imaginary line. They favour 'simple' parries rather than the circular ones of the Italians – perhaps because they feel

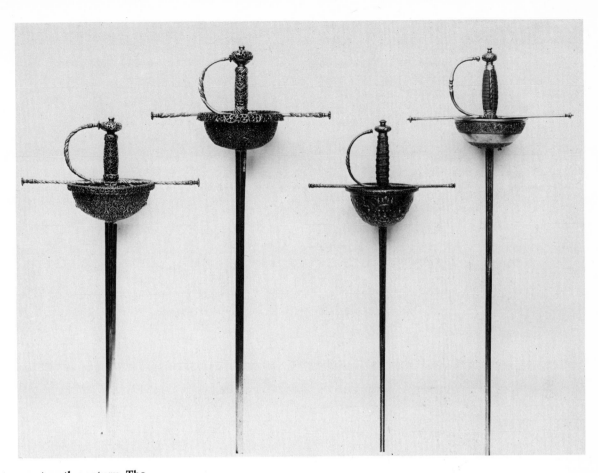

er variants of the seventeenth century. The
cup-hilted weapons are Spanish. The shell-
d weapon is Flemish and the weapon with the
le 'dish' guard, quillons and knuckle-bow is
nan. Victoria and Albert Museum.

1   **The *botte du paysan* advocated by La Touche.
From *La Spada Maestra* by Bondi di Mazo.**

2 & 3   **Italian positions in rapier play in the last quarter of
the seventeenth century. From *Regole della
Scherma* by Marcelli.**

1

that the simple is more secure, perhaps because
they consider the circular might take a fraction
more time. They do not approve of sidestepping
to avoid an attack, but they are prepared to teach
it under popular pressure. Equally they teach the
occasional use of the left hand whilst not entirely
approving of it. They teach the disarm – the
removal of the opponent's sword from his grasp,
usually by seizing it and wrenching it from him –
because it was still considered useful in combat.
Liancour favours the occasional use of a 'universal' parry – a rapid, circular movement of the
point covering the whole of the target – for there
were, after all, still many dark alleys in the Europe
of the late seventeenth century, just as there were
shady characters to lurk in them. And Liancour
also throws interesting light on the need for a
master of fence to preserve his status and authority, by recommending that the pupil be given a
practice weapon both heavier and shorter than
that of his master. A difference to which, no doubt,
the pupil's attention was not drawn.

But a man instructed by these French masters
and in possession of the small sword of the late
seventeenth century was one of the deadliest
opponents that personal combat has ever seen.

2

3

Parade de la pointe au dedans des armes. ✦ *Le coup qu'il faut a cette parade*

Parade du fort au dehors des armes. ✦ *Le coup a ceux qui parent en esleuant leur espee.*

Parade de la pointe au dehors des armes. ✦ *Le coup qu'il faut a cette parade.*

Flanconnade. ✦ *Demie volte du corps.*

Coup donné a ceux qui parēt en abaiss.^t le bras. ❦ *Coup dōné a ceux qui parēt en esleuant le bras.*

Parade de l'espée que l'on tient des deux mains ❦ *Le coup qu'il faut donner.*

Passe de quarte au dedans des armes
au pied droit leué. ❦ *Passe de tierce au dessus des armes*
au pied gauche leué.

Passe de seconde dessous les armes. ❦ *Saisisement d'espée.*

The small sword fight as taught by Liancour. A comparison with the illustrations from Fabris is interesting. Almost all features of early rapier play have disappeared. The guards and parries are clearly established. The left hand is used only rarely. There is no trace of that circular pattern of fight that characterised early play with the rapier (see also pages 136 and 137).

Following pages
Top
Liancour's view of the Italian small sword fight.
Below
Liancour's view of the German small sword fight.
From *Le Maistre d'Armes.*

6 Marcelli; 7 Liancour; 8 Agrippa; 9 Thibault.

6

8

7

9

Chapter Seven

THE PERFECTION OF THEORY AND PRACTICE

The seventeenth century in Europe saw a mounting body of legislation against personal combat. Baldick recalls that 'no fewer than ten edicts restraining the practice' were issued during the reign of Louis XIV in France, without any real success. Despite the edict of 1679 'which prescribed the death penalty for all principals, seconds, and thirds, with greater or less confiscation of property' and 'ordained that gentlemen should be deprived of their letters of nobility: and their coats of arms defaced and broken by the public executioner; and ruled that those who fell in a duel should be tried by contumacy, and their bodies deprived of Christian burial', men still persisted in calling one another out on the slightest of pretexts. Personal combat, it seems, gave some distinction to a man. A man who had killed another had in some way 'proved' himself. He was held in a certain awe. He held a certain magic for the ladies.

But despite the glamour with which such combat was invested, we should not be blind to the bloody nature of it. In England, in spite of proclamations and ordinances against personal combat issued by James and Cromwell, the practice continued. The second Earl of Chesterfield was imprisoned in the Tower under the Protectorate for wounding Captain Whaly in a fight with swords. In 1667, Pepys talks of the fight between the two friends Bellasses and Porter. Porter had declared that he would like to see the man in England 'that durst give me a blow', whereupon Bellasses had struck him with his hand. Porter was determined to fight, stopped Bellasses' coach 'and bade Sir H. Bellasses come out':

'"Why," said Sir H. Bellasses, "you will not hurt me coming out, will you?" – "No," says Tom Porter. So out he went, and both drew. And Sir H. Bellasses having drawn and flung away the scabbard, Tom Porter asked him whether he was ready. The other answered, he was; and they fell to fight, some of their acquaintances by. They wounded one another; and Sir H. Bellasses so much, that it is

The guards recommended by Sir William Hope for small sword play.

The guard of quarte recommended by Hope, compared with that used in French small sword play. From *The Compleat Fencing Master.*

The duel between the Duke of Hamilton and Lord Mohun, November 1712.

feared he will die. And finding himself severely wounded, he called to Tom Porter, and kissed him, and bade him shift for himself; "for," says he, "Tom thou hast hurt me; but I will make shift to stand on my legs till thou mayest withdraw, and the world not take notice of thee; for I would not have thee troubled for what thou hast done." And so, whether he did fly or not, I cannot tell; but Tom Porter showed Sir H. Bellasses that he was wounded too; and they are both ill, but Sir H. Bellasses to the life.'

There is a touch of romance about the affair. But there is none in the meeting between Lord Mohun and the Duke of Hamilton which took place in Hyde Park late in 1712. Nor is there any of that style and finesse advocated by the French masters of small-sword play in their schools. The encounter was brief, savage and bloody. Swift says of it:

'This morning, at eight, my man brought me word that Duke Hamilton had fought with Lord Mohun, and had killed him, and was brought home wounded. I immediately sent him to the Duke's house to know if it was so, but the porter could hardly answer his inquiries, and a great rabble was about the house. In short, they fought at seven this morning. The dog Mohun was killed on the spot, but while the Duke was over him, Mohun shortened his sword and stabbed him in the shoulder to the heart. The Duke was helped towards the lake-house, by the ring, in Hyde Park (where they fought), and died on the grass, before he could reach his house, and was brought home in his coach by eight, while the poor Duchess was asleep. Maccartney and one Hamilton were the seconds, who fought likewise, and both are fled. I am told that a footman of Lord Mohun's stabbed Duke Hamilton, and some say Maccartney did too. Mohun gave the affront, and yet sent the challenge. I am infinitely concerned for the poor Duke, who was a frank, honest, and good natured man.'

George Lockhart is clearer about what happened

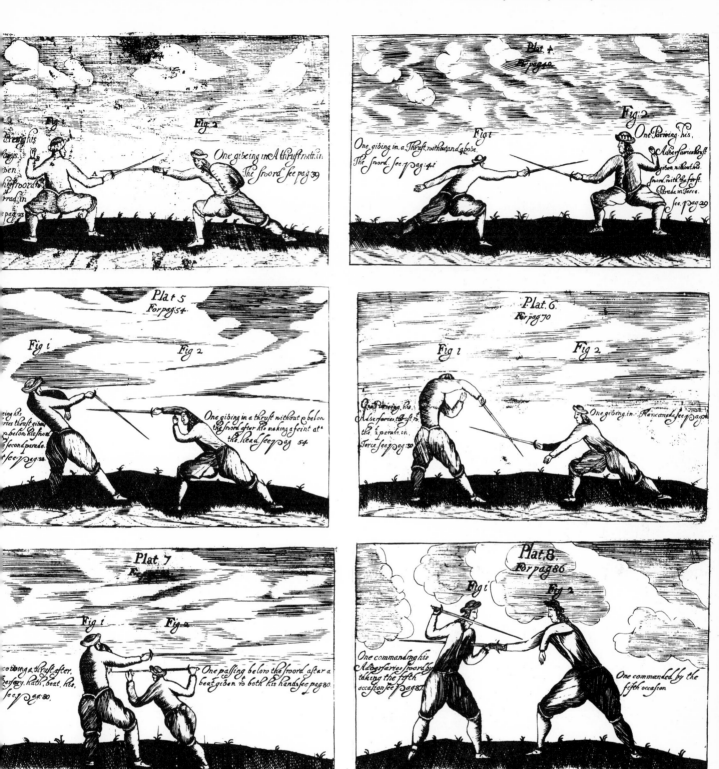

... style of small sword play recommended by
... e. From *The Compleat Fencing Master*.

The style of small sword play recommended by Hope (*continued*).

and about the political motivation of the affair. The Duke, he says, had Colonel John Hamilton as his second. The second for Mohun was 'General McKertny':

'All four immediately fell to work, and Hamiltoun having soon disarmed McKertny and looking about to see what was become of the other two, he perceivd Mohun lying dead or expiring on his back, and the Duke falln on his face on the top of the other. Then throwing down his own and McKertny's swords, he ran and lifted up the Duke, who he observ'd was wounded in two places, and faint with the effusion of blood from the wound in his thigh. Whilst he was performing this good office, McKertny took up one of the swords, and coming behind Hamiltoun, whilst he supported the Duke by the back in his arms, stabbd His Grace, who walked nevertheless some litle way to a tree, where he soon after expir'd, and as soon as the keepers of the Park and some others came up, which was just as the Duke reacht the tree, McKertny went off. This account Hamiltoun gave of the matter; but the Whigs took a world of pains to save McKertny's reputation and person, by denying that part which the second did averr he had acted, and hiding him so carefully, that, tho all means were us'd to discover him, he was securely conceald and at length safely conveyd beyond sea.'

The 'unbyass'd part of mankind', says Lockhart, 'did credit Hamiltoun's account, believing that the Dukes death was a wilful premeditated murder.'

'It was impossible for my Lord Mohun to give the Duke the wound which killd him, for he was run in at the very top of the left breast, near to the collar bone, sloping down so far towards his belly, that had the wound been but an inch or two deeper, it had pierc'd his belly above his navel; and Mohun cou'd not plant such a thrust, unless he had stood up very high above

Below
The guard with the small sword when opposing the broadsword man. From Hope's *The Compleat Fencing Master*.

Following pages
The mounted pistol exercise. The illustrations support Hope's description of the complexity of pistol combat on horseback. From Grose's *Military Antiquities*.

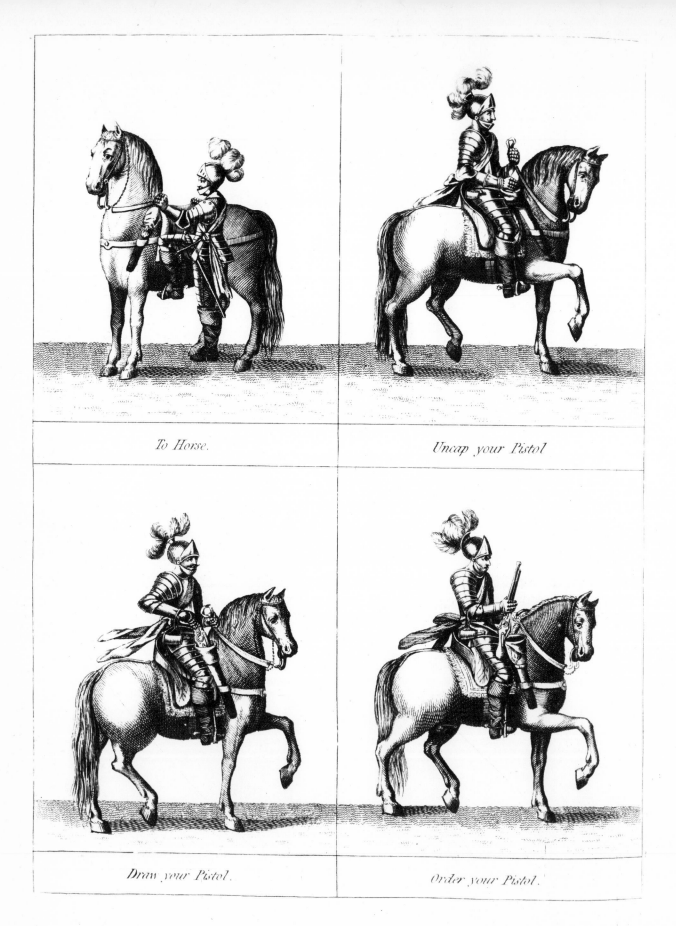

To Horse.

Uncap your Pistol

Draw your Pistol.

Order your Pistol.

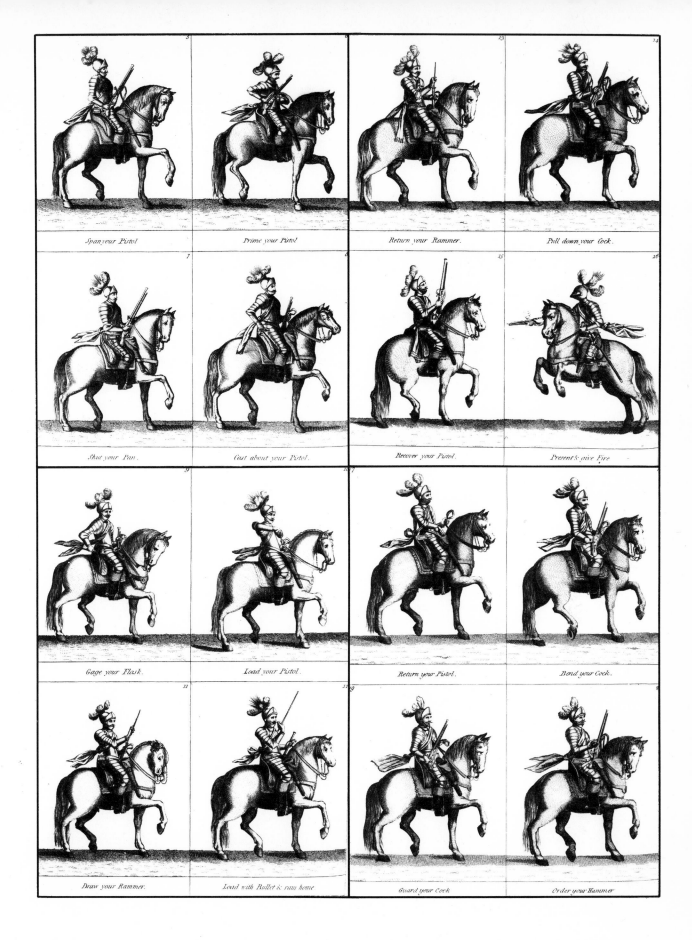

Span your Pistol

Prime your Pistol.

Return your Rammer.

Pull down your Cock.

Shut your Pan.

Cast about your Pistol.

Recover your Pistol.

Present & give Fire

Gage your Flask.

Load your Pistol.

Return your Pistol.

Bend your Cock.

Draw your Rammer.

Load with Bullet & ram home

Guard your Cock

Order your Hammer

Small sword play as experienced by Donald McBane. From *The Expert Swordsman's Companion.*

the duke, or having enclos'd had shortened his sword' (the *botte du paysan* of La Touche).

The opinion of a certain Doctor Garth confirms Lockhart's view. 'It was impossible', Garth said, 'for my Lord Mohun to grapple and give that wound to the Duke, after he himself had receivd the wound of which he died.'

'But to put the matter out of all controversy [says Lockhart] the sword which was found in Mohun's hand, and known to be what he usually wore, was a Saxon blade, wheras the wound in the Duke's body, wherof he died, was with a three corner blade, which, being the only one of that amongst them, belong'd to Hamiltoun, and was snatcht up by McKertny to perpetrate the execrable deed.'

And of the political motivation of the affair, Lockhart says, 'I have been more particular in the account of this dismal story, that it may thence appear, there's too much ground to believe the Whigs are a set of men, who stand at nothing to accomplish their own ends.'

Both these fights were between members of the 'upper' class, and it is interesting to see the extent to which the small sword became increasingly identified with that class. Other members of society favoured other weapons. 'Every man claiming gentry', says Aylward of the early years of the eighteenth century, 'wore the small sword at his side.' Yet still the old weapons persisted in one combat or another – the back-sword, sword and dagger, sword and buckler, single fauchion, case of fauchions, quarterstaff, pike and the two-handed sword. To see them in public use meant a visit to one of the gladiatorial combats which persisted in their popularity well into the eighteenth century.

Sir William Hope of Scotland made an attempt, with some success, to tread a path of compromise between the old styles and the old weapons, and the new French fight with the small sword. This is perhaps not surprising. He was a man of culture,

with the background of a practising soldier. He was Deputy Governor of Edinburgh Castle, where he would be well aware of the old traditions. And he was an amateur, and therefore presumably not involved in professional squabbles concerning the merits of a particular style on which his livelihood depended. In many ways he is a later version of George Silver, vigorous, passionate, perhaps a little eccentric.

Hope recommends regular practice above all else. Despite the fact that he set his own theories down in no less than eight books during the period 1687–1725, 'what will that avail a Man, when he is either to make use of Blunts or Sharps?' he asks. 'Theorie without Practice will signifie but for little, therefore fall to the practising of your lessons on the Fencing-Master's Breast.' He recommends, too, that that same fencing master should not simply be proficient in the small sword, but also in the back-sword, the cutting weapon. And he has his eye always on the true purpose behind practice, the occasion on which a man's life would depend on it: 'make them Assault sometimes in their ordinary Shoes and Clothes, as also sometimes in the open Fields when the weather is good, a most useful Thing when a Man comes to be engaged for his Life.'

But despite this stress on the practice of swordplay as a preparation for actual combat, Hope records that never once in his life was he involved in such a situation. No doubt this accounts for his academic strictures on some moves which in actual combat must have had their uses. Surprisingly, for example, he derides attacks on the arms and legs. Yet in actual combat the cut at the inside of the right wrist was regarded as one of the most effective ways of incapacitating an opponent, and a thrust through the opponent's advanced knee could stop any fight. He dislikes the use of the left hand for parrying or creating an opening, and he forbids the technique of allowing the grip on the sword to be changed during the course of a thrust despite the fact that such a move could increase the reach by three or four inches. He is, at bottom, an academic theorist who was never

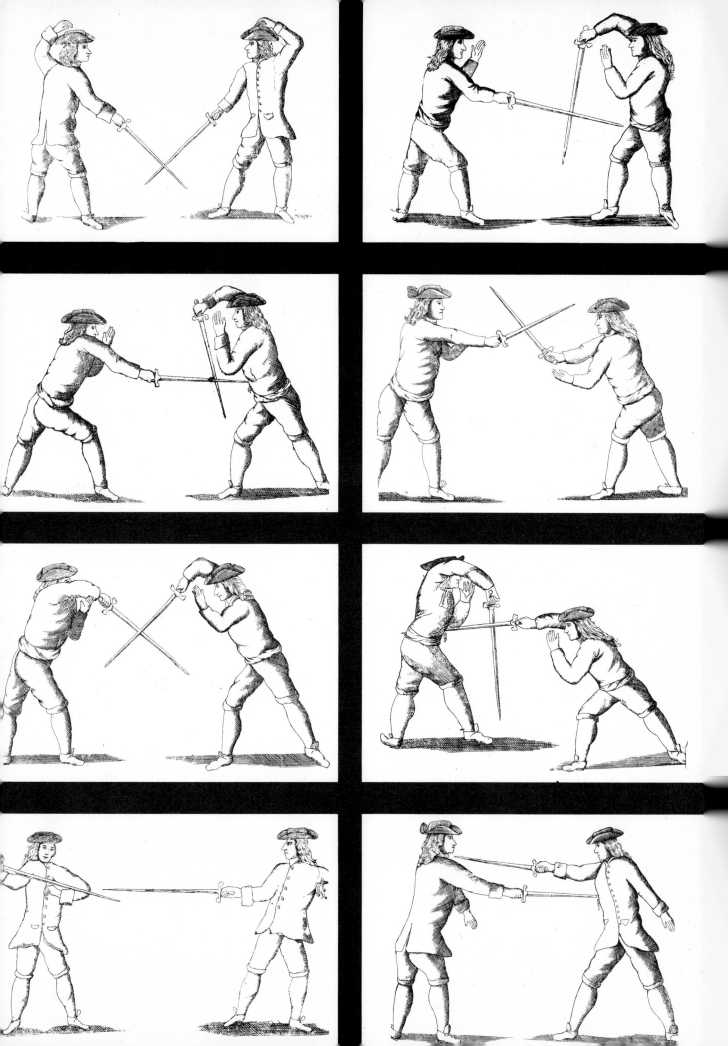

1 The 'Boar's Thrust', the movement that McBane favoured for killing an opponent with the small sword.

2 McBane's guard for the fight with broadswords.

3 The guard recommended by McBane for the small sword and dagger fight or the fight with a 'case' of small swords. From *The Expert Swordsman's Companion.*

called upon to put his principles seriously to the test. But he is important because his works were widely read, and many men must have engaged in real combat equipped with his theories and practice.

Hope deals mainly with the small sword as being, in his view, the most fit weapon for the gentleman. But he is aware of other weapons which the gentleman might find opposing him. Against the back-sword and shearing sword – against which he has no doubt that the small sword will ultimately triumph – he advocates a defensive technique. The man with the cutting weapon is to be allowed to attack, the attack is to be avoided and the attacker at once run through the middle by the small-sword man. And despite his disapproval of attacks on arms and legs, he is sufficiently realistic to warn his reader of the cutting technique of attacking the inside of the sword-wrist.

3

We see in Hope the beginning of the end of sword-play as the most efficient way of killing a man. Hope demonstrates that it is possible to be a nationally recognised authority, without ever being called upon to put theory to the test. In him, sword-play begins to be something more than preparation for combat; it becomes something that can be practised for its own sake. And he mentions a factor that was assuming increasing importance in combat, the use of the pistol. If, as Castle said, 'the development of the "Art of Fence" was the result of the invention of fire-arms', then the end of that art for combat purposes arose from the same cause. Hope heralds that end, although the actual discarding of the sword in serious combat was still many years off. Hope gives an indication of the general inaccuracy and inefficiency of the pistol at the beginning of the eighteenth century, in his instructions on pistol fighting on horseback:

'Draw your right Pistol, and bending her, put her into your Bridle Hand, holding her near the Work with your foremost Finger and Thumb. Then immediately draw your

Gladiatorial combat with the quarterstaff, according
to James Miller.

1 The swords used in gladiatorial combat.

2 The attack with the point on the swordarm, coinciding with an opponent's attack, according to James Miller.

Following pages
Formal military pike drill, an exercise that must have formed part of Donald McBane's training as a professional fighting man. From Grose's *Military Antiquities*.

left, and holding her in your right hand, keep her Muzzle upwards. Now turn your Horse, and come at a Hand Gallop until you be within a Pair, or less, of your Adversary, keeping still up the Muzzle of your Pistol. When you are about a Pair from him, make a brusch close by him so that you may almost touch his Legg, letting your Pistol fall by Degrees so that in passing you may almost touch him with it, then fire upon him. If your Pistol be in order as she should, will hardly ever fail to do Execution.'

The distance between the two combatants at the moment of discharge must have been no more than three feet, and yet such was the inefficiency of the pistol that even at that range one might miss! In which case, says Hope:

'Immediately you are past him, drop the Pistol you fired, and take the Pistol which is already cocked in your Left-hand into your Right, change your Horse to the Right, and so Gallop on untill you be at a Pair again with your Adversary, and then behave just as you did with your first Pistol.'

It should be noted that the horsemen also carry the sword. In the incredible, but apparently not uncommon, event of all four pistols missing their marks, then they could go at one another with the point!

The pistol that Hope had in mind was an early flintlock, heavy, ill-balanced and unreliable. It had to be charged correctly, the touch-hold had to be cleaned, it had to be primed, and the flint in the jaws had to be capable of producing the necessary ignition without fail. It was still some considerable time before such a weapon became sufficiently reliable for men to prefer it in combat to the sword.

Donald McBane – a Scotsman like Hope – gives us perhaps the finest picture that exists of the life of a European professional fighter during the latter part of the seventeenth and the early years of the eighteenth centuries. He is in many

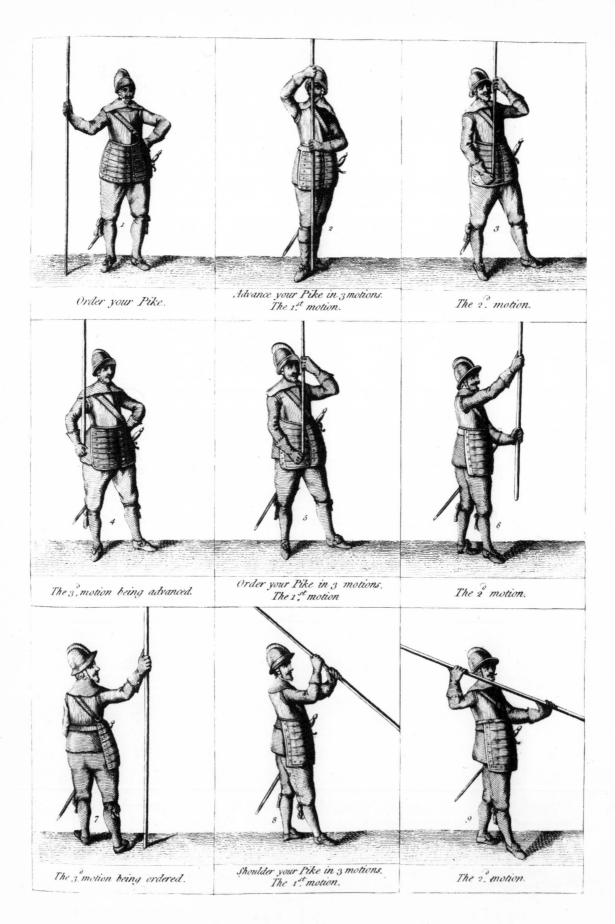

Order your Pike.

Advance your Pike in 3 motions.
The 1st motion.

The 2d motion.

The 3d motion being advanced.

Order your Pike in 3 motions.
The 1st motion

The 2d motion.

The 3d motion being ordered.

Shoulder your Pike in 3 motions.
The 1st motion.

The 2d motion.

The 3.ᵈ motion being Shouldered.

Port your Pike in 3 motions.
The 1.ˢᵗ motion.

The 2. motion.

The 3.ᵈ motion being Ported.

Charge your Pike.

Advance your Pike.

Shoulder your Pike in 3 motions.
The 1.ˢᵗ motion.

The 2.ᵈ motion.

The 3.ᵈ motion being Shouldered.

Charge to the Rear in 3 motions.
The 1.ˢᵗ motion.

The 2.ᵈ motion.

The 3.ᵈ motion being charged.

Recover your Pike & Shoulder in 3 motioⁿˢ.
The 1.ˢᵗ motion.

The 2.ᵈ motion.

The 3.ᵈ motion being Shoulder'd.

Order your Pike.

Cheeke your Pike
The 1.ˢᵗ motion.

The 2.ᵈ motion being Cheek'd.

The inevitable outcome of most sword duels in the eighteenth century. The duel has taken place within the security of a private room from which the victor is seen escaping through the window. The illustration shows very clearly the lethal nature of the eighteenth-century small-sword with its narrow, stiff blade and needle-sharp point. The victim has been struck through the left breast, a wound which will almost certainly prove fatal. *The Killing of the Earl*. From *Marriage à la Mode* by Hogarth in the National Gallery, London.

Trayle your Pike.

Recover your Pike and Charge
The 1.ˢᵗ Palming motion

The 2.ᵈ Palming motion.

Charge your Pike.

Order at close order.

Put up your Sword & order your Pike.

1 Small sword play in the first quarter of the eighteenth century: the disarm by seizure of the opponent's weapon. From Blackwell's *The Gentleman's Tutor*.

2 The grip prior to drawing the sword. From Angelo's *Ecole des Armes*.

I

ways the antithesis of Sir William Hope. Hope was a gentleman, McBane was not. Hope had a commission, McBane served in the ranks. Hope never experienced personal combat himself, whereas McBane seems to have been engaged in one bout after another. In his early combats he worked on a trial-and-error basis, since he had had no training. In his first contest with a fellow soldier, arising from a dispute over pay, he was disarmed. But he made a second attempt, was successful, and had to flee.

In Ireland, deciding that personal combat was something he must take seriously, he took lessons and as a result opened a school of fence of his own. He saw service in the Low Countries under Marlborough and opened a string of fencing schools-cum-brothels in collaboration with his wife. To establish one of them, in Brabant, he had to fight twenty-four times himself, before his competitors could be persuaded to accept him. As an example of the problems that he constantly faced in setting up one of his fencing 'establishments', he mentions his experience in Friedberg in the summer of 1704:

'We set up all sorts of gaming Tents, we had not above sixty Campaign Ladies in the Quarters. Sixteen Professors of the Sword resolved to go to the Emperor's Quarters (Prince Eugene's) where we got fourteen brave Dutch Lasses as a reinforcement. Next day came twenty-four Swordsmen and demanded the Ladies again. We had a drink, fought Two and Two, eleven Dutch killed and seven of our Men. I fought eight running, we buried our Dead and parted.'

When he left the army he set up still another school of fence and took to gladiatorial fighting. He fought thirty-seven times in the period of two years. His last fight was at the age of sixty-three in Edinburgh, when battered and scarred from old fights and with a silver plate in his head, he gave his challenger 'seven Wounds, and broke his Arm with the Fauchion'.

1 & 2   Coming on guard so as to defend the 'inside' or the
'outside' of the target.

3 – 7   The formal salute taught by Angelo.

1

3

2

5

The guards and the principal direct attacks taught by Angelo.

His principal caution to a would-be combatant is, 'Trust nobody'. A fighting man should be on his guard at all times. Hang the punctilio of the French masters, the rules of decent combat, the behaviour of gentlemen; when a man is putting his life at stake, the only rule is success. Never turn your back on an opponent – or indeed on a man with whom you've quarrelled. Never accept his statement that you have defeated him until you have his sword in your hand. Never accept a defeated opponent's sword from him unless it is given to you hilt first. In his experience he has met opponents who have thrown their hats in his face in the middle of a fight, men who have thrown their swords, point first like javelins, and men who have taken up a handful of earth and tossed it in his eyes. Some made a practice of carrying earth in their pockets for this purpose; others concealed a small pistol in their hats. His own special thrust, when he has decided to kill a man, is to drop his sword-hand from the level of his waist to his knee, at the same time thrusting upwards under his opponent's guard. Descriptively, he calls it the 'Boar's Thrust'.

Aylward gives an admirable summary of McBane's style:

'Arrived on the field, the coat must be taken off and the gloves put on. The handle of one's sword should be just so thick that the little finger can be closed round it so as to touch the palm; if it is larger, a man is disarmed easily by a heavy beat on the blade. 'After Points are presented, you must take care of yourself, for there's no Time given.' Traverse continually, keep in constant motion, and never allow the enemy to feel the blade. The left hand should be held above the left eye, and it is essential that all thrusts should be parried with it, but a most useful dodge is to hold one's cane or scabbard by the middle with the left hand, parrying with it instead of with the gloved palm.

'The guard advised by Donald McBane is with the point close to the opponent's shell [the shell-shaped guard of the eighteenth-century small sword], threatening his hand, "but not within his shell, lest he seize your point and break it". Half-thrusts should be made at the hand, wrist, and arm, but never beyond the elbow for "if you prick him, he will go out of line and leave an open at his body". It is a mistake to lunge out, a half-lunge is all that is needed, for four or five inches of steel discourage an adversary just as much as a thrust clean through the body. After a lunge, the swordsman must recover instantly, jumping back out of distance if he can. If the enemy falls back to avoid being hit, the left foot must be brought up to the right, and the fencer must fall on guard again.

'The best mode of attack is to start with beats on the blade, followed by single or double feints not pushed home, but intended to worry the enemy. If he draws back, he may be followed cautiously, with continual half-thrusts at the hand and forearm, in the hope of getting an opening. But Donald's serious advice is that it is far less dangerous to retire than to advance "and not at all scandalous", as it is generally believed, seeing that a retreat gives an opportunity for a time-hit on the adversary's advance, though one must beware of a counter-time'.

Although McBane regards the small sword as the nearest thing to perfection, it is probably the spadroon, with its flat blade, sharp edge and point, that he most frequently fought with. In facing a small-sword man with such a weapon, he recommends an attack with the edge on his extended wrist. His approach is cautious, simple, eminently practical. He advances no theories that he has not himself tried out and found successful in actual combat.

Another practitioner in Britain at the time McBane was writing was Captain J. Miller. He was the James Miller, then sergeant, who had fought Timothy Buck at back-sword on Monday 21 July 1712 at the Bear Garden at Hockley-in-the-Hole, and would have fought him also, according to the challenge, with 'Sword and Dagger, Sword and Buckler, Single Fauchion,

Case of Fauchions and Quarterstaff', had he not been severely wounded in the left leg. Steele, writing in the *Spectator* (no. 436), described him as:

'A man of six foot eight inches height, of a kind but bold aspect, well fashioned, and ready of his limbs, and such a readiness as spoke his ease in them was obtained from military exercise'.

And of the fight itself, Steele continues:

'It is not easy to describe the many escapes and imperceptible defences between two men of quick eyes and ready limbs, but Miller's heat laid him open to the rebuke of the calm Buck by a large cut on the forehead. As soon as his wound was wrapped up, he came on again with a little rage, which disabled him further. But what brave man can be wounded into more patience and caution?

'The next was a warm eager onset, which ended in a decisive stroke on the left leg of Miller. The wound was exposed to the view of all who could delight in it, and sewed up on the stage.'

The illustrations from Miller's brief treatise on fighting with the sword show the weapons still in use in Britain at the time. They supplement the statements made in Captain John Godfrey's book, *A Treatise upon the useful Science of Defence*, which first appeared in 1747.

The pinnacle of British eighteenth-century theory and practice was reached with the work of the Angelos, and in particular with the first of them, Domenico. Domenico was born in Leghorn in 1717, the eldest son of a merchant. He studied the Italian method in Pisa, and the French method under Teillagory – reputedly the greatest swordsman in France – in Paris. Beginning as a specialist in equitation, he was persuaded to open a school of fence which he established at Carlisle House in 1763. There can be no doubt about his skill with the small

The defence with the small sword in the second
half of the eighteenth century: the parries taught by
Angelo.

Methods of riposting with the small sword immediately after the completion of a successful parry.

1 A disengagement from the guard of quarte by cutting over the top of the opposing blade.

2 The attack following the disengagement by cut-over, made by 'passing' – stepping forward with the left foot instead of lunging.

sword. He had demolished Redman, whom he had succeeded as riding and fencing master to George, Prince of Wales, and Edward, Duke of York, with his cane in the Haymarket, and he had 'planted half a dozen perfect hits' on Dr Keyes, the leading Irish amateur, in the presence of a distinguished company, without having been touched himself.

His method is not original, nor could it be. There was little that could be said to advance small-sword play after the work of Liancour and Labat. But it is sound and methodical, and it is still based on the premise that, although fencing was rapidly becoming simply an elegant accomplishment of gentlemen, the ultimate purpose of practice with the sword was the possibility of serious combat. In consequence, Angelo teaches various methods of disarming an opponent, and in certain circumstances he thinks the use of the left hand, in controlling the opponent's blade, legitimate. He teaches the circular parry, which the early French masters had thought too insecure and slow, but which Hope had thought effective some fifty years earlier. He thinks the 'circle-parade' – the universal parry of so many earlier masters – useful in a tight corner, and advocates thrusting at the face in serious combat in case one's opponent should be wearing some form of protection under the coat. The relationship that Angelo still sees between sword practice and actual combat is shown by the fact that he still thinks it necessary to deal with such combinations as the sword and dagger, sword and cloak and sword and lantern – that particularly nasty technique of assassins by which an opponent was dazzled in some dark alley by having the light of a lantern shone full in his face, and at the same time run through with the sword. Angelo was perhaps remembering the time in Paris when he was ambushed in the dark. Armed only with a short hunting sword he defeated his attacker, though the man was found later to have been wearing a mail shirt under his coat.

Angelo's theories were not put to serious test as frequently as current popular opinion would

suggest. James Gilchrist, in his *A Brief Display of the Origin and History of Ordeals* (London, 1821), is able to trace only 172 formal duels, in which 69 fighters were killed and 48 seriously wounded. There must have been many informal encounters, and formal encounters that were never given any publicity. In other European countries, the situation seems to have been different. Harry Angelo – Domenico's son – writing of his experiences in Paris about the year 1780, says that the Frenchman would draw his sword with as much alacrity as an Englishman would put up his fists. English law may have had something to do with it. It recognised the 'rencounter' as being different from the 'duel'. The rencounter took place at the same time as the offence; it took place in a momentary passion and was therefore not premeditated. Death in a rencounter was regarded as manslaughter. The duel was different. There was a lapse of time between the offence and the fight that was to remedy it. There was a cooling-off period. Any fight that took place after that period did so in cold blood. It was premeditated, and a death resulting from such a meeting was regarded as murder.

Nevertheless, some of Angelo's pupils did appear in duels. John Wilkes, a friend of Angelo's and almost certainly one of his pupils, was editor of the *North Briton*. Articles published in the periodical were the cause of his engagements. He met the Earl of Talbot in the garden of the Red Lion at Bagshot in 1762. Talbot insisted on fighting with horse-pistols rather than swords. Shots were fired but neither man was harmed. Pistols, it seems, were no more accurate in Angelo's early days than they had been when Hope recommended the method of using them some fifty years previously. In 1763 another piece in the *North Briton* brought a challenge from Samuel Martin, Member of Parliament for Camelford. The encounter took place in Hyde Park. Again it was with pistols and again neither man was hit on the first exchange of shots. But on the second exchange Wilkes' pistol misfired and he took Martin's bullet in the stomach. The

1

2

1 Counters to the attack on the lunge and the attack by 'passing', made by displacement of the body.

2 Techniques of disarming an opponent in small sword play.

1

wound was not serious. It seems to have been deflected by a button on Wilkes' waistcoat and did no more than score the surface of the flesh. It provides an interesting comment on the effectiveness of the pistol as a weapon of personal combat at that time: of the four shots fired from close range, only one struck its target and that with such little force that it was deflected by a waistcoat button, resulting in a wound that was only superficial.

The case of Lieutenant Riddle, a friend of the Angelo family, is less happy. He had studied the sword under Angelo, but when he fought his duel with Lieutenant Cunningham of the Scots Greys he chose to do so with pistols. Cunningham forced the fight on Riddle after some trivial quarrel over cards. Riddle fired first at a distance of eight paces. His ball struck Cunningham in the chest. But Cunningham did not fall. After a pause he fired at Riddle and hit him in the groin. Riddle died a few hours later. Cunningham was dead a day or two afterwards, and so avoided being brought to trial for manslaughter.

Richard Brinsley Sheridan, the playwright, a close friend of the Angelos, fought two duels with the small sword against a Captain Matthews. The provocation followed a familiar pattern. Matthews, a married man, was pestering a Miss Linley, who was later to become Sheridan's wife. Sheridan intervened to protect her. As a result of Sheridan's interference, Matthews put a highly scurrilous piece in the *Bath Chronicle* attacking Sheridan's character. Sheridan forced a fight upon him. Matthews was unhappy about the affair. Sheridan was only twenty. Matthews had had years of experience in the army and in the fencing schools. Whatever the outcome, Matthews was bound to be regarded in an unfavourable light. The fight took place eventually in an upper room at the Castle Tavern in Henrietta Street, London, by the light of candles. Despite Matthews' experience, Sheridan disarmed him by beating his blade, seizing his hilt and threatening him with the point of his sword –

2

Disarming an opponent.

The frontispiece from Captain Sinclair's book, *Cudgel-playing Modernised and Improved*. Despite the fact that Sinclair was writing at the end of the eighteenth century the illustration is typical of the gladiators who fought in public some sixty years earlier. The sword, with its complete protection for the hand, has a blade reminiscent of the cavalry cutting weapon of the seventeenth century. The shield as a defensive instrument in serious personal combat had disappeared many years earlier. The posture adopted by Sinclair suggests those that appear in Meyer's work of two centuries earlier and like those seems to be an attempt to emulate Mars himself. From the copy in the possession of the National Library of Scotland, Edinburgh.

A duel with flintlock pistols, with seconds, judge and physician in attendance. The signal to fire, in this particular case, has been given by the dropping of a handkerchief. Such a signal was designed to make it more difficult for the duellist to hit his opponent since it was argued that the combatants could not keep their eyes on the handkerchief and the targets at which they were aiming at one and the same time. The positions of the two principals here are interesting. The one on the right has adopted almost the classic position for duelling with the pistol, with a sideways stance designed to reduce the size of the target he presents. By contrast his opponent, with his left foot advanced, has taken up a squarer body position and so increased the size of the target. From a nineteenth-century print.

CAPT. G. SINCLAIR.

A small sword of 1781, made in London and presented to Colonel James Hartley by the East India Company. Victoria and Albert Museum.

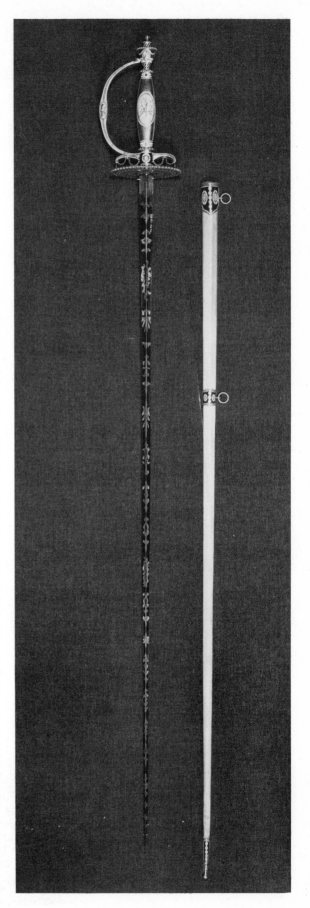

a move straight out of the old rapier play, one that was condemned by many masters of the period and yet one which was still highly effective. It brought the fight to an end, without either party being injured.

News of Matthews' defeat by the much younger and less experienced man leaked out. To save face, Matthews was forced to challenge Sheridan again. The engagement took place early on the morning of 8 July 1772, at Kings Weston near Bath. Despite the great advances in theory and academic practice that had taken place since the days of Marozzo we can still see, in this second Sheridan-Matthews fight, that when men intended serious injury to one another – even in the late eighteenth century – the cool logic of the fencing school was very soon abandoned. After a few passes, Matthews succeeded in tripping his opponent, and fell upon him on the ground. Aylward summarises the contest in this way:

'The older and stronger man, and the more experienced swordsman, Matthews drove Sheridan back until, at last, the latter tried to bring off the trick which had been so effective in London: attempting to come to close quarters and to lay hold of Matthews' sword. But taught by experience, and perhaps counselled beforehand by his expert second (an Irishman, William Barnett), Matthews fell back, and "received Sheridan upon his point".

'After this the conflict ceased to have any relation to the art of fence; Matthews seized Sheridan by the arm, and a struggle ensued in which both men came to the ground, their swords being broken in the fall. At this point the seconds ought to have interfered, but they allowed the two combatants to continue the scuffle, hitting and stabbing at each other with their broken blades. It ended by Matthews getting on top of Sheridan, and nailing him to the ground by thrusting his broken point through the skin of his opponent's neck, after which he took to his waiting post-chaise and made off to London. Although a good deal knocked about, Sheridan was not seriously hurt, and he recovered after a lengthy convalescence; months later Harry Angelo noticed that the wound in the neck "still looked very sore".'

Angelo is certainly the most important figure in British personal combat theory in the eighteenth century. Yet in many ways he heralded the end of such combat with the sword. There was no more efficient thrusting weapon for killing a man than the small sword and in consequence there were few ways in which the theory and practice of its use could be developed further. And, as we have seen, a totally new method of kill-ing a man was being evolved. The pistol, towards the end of the eighteenth century, was still a crude and unreliable weapon, but it already contained within itself the idea of thrusting a hole through an opponent far more effectively than could be done with the small sword, and without coming into close personal contact with him. And it had another great virtue: to be profi-cient with the small sword required long practice – three years had been suggested as the minimum – but proficiency with the pistol, at what nowa-days we would regard as almost point-blank range, required no more than an ability to load it correctly, aim it accurately and pull the trigger.

The small sword and cloak opposed to the small
sword and lantern.

The movements of the salute with the French small sword according to Girard.

The small sword fight taught by Girard.

Les deux troisi.° et dernieres attitudes du salut d'armes. 12.
4.° planche.

6.° attitude. 5.° attitude.

25. *Coup de flanconnade sur le flanc.*
12.° planche.

Voyés la parade de ce coup a la planche suivante, et page 38. &c.

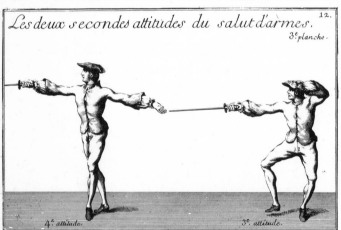

Les deux secondes attitudes du salut d'armes. 12.
3.° planche.

4.° attitude. 3.° attitude.

71. *Passe de quarte, au dedans des armes.*
36.° planche.

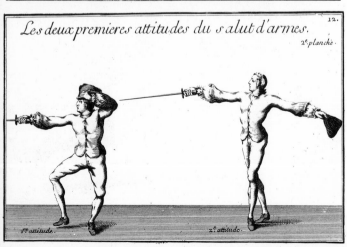

Les deux premieres attitudes du salut d'armes. 12.
2.° planche.

1.° attitude. 2.° attitude.

87. *Parade de ceux qui tiennent leur Epée a deux mains.*
53.° planche.

b   a

Voyés le coup frapé planche suivante.

Chapter Eight

THE DECLINE OF THE SWORD

In continental Europe, the eighteenth-century development of personal combat is similar to that that we have seen in England and Scotland. The small sword, used according to the principles of Liancour and Labat, continued to dominate the scene of upper-class combat, whilst elsewhere other weapons were in use. Le Sieur Girard brought out in 1730 'the most splendid work on fencing, with the exception of Angelo's, that ever appeared since Thibault's ponderous folio'. Girard was a retired naval officer, and a practitioner as well as a theorist. He deals with the small sword, as one would expect, but he also deals with it in opposition to the broadsword, the pike and the spontoon. The small sword had continued to lighten since the days of Labat, for Girard now recommends those circular parries that Labat had considered too slow and unreliable.

Danet, writing in 1787, makes what is really the final pronouncement on the French method of fighting with the small sword. He advocates only one guard and he disapproves of all 'dodging' instead of parrying. But since he still has his eye on the use of the small sword in personal combat, rather than exclusively in the fencing salon, he admits that in serious fighting it might still have its place. So, too, might the 'parade de cercle' – Angelo's 'circle parade', the 'universal' parry for use in a tight corner.

But small-sword play as the universal answer to the question, 'How do I kill my opponent?', was past its heyday. Practice in the 'schools' had become 'academic' and 'artificial'. 'The fear of wounding an adversary in the school, which would have disgraced a fencer for life, could not act otherwise than detrimentally on his velocity of movement, however it might tend to keep up his *form*', says Castle. 'How different a "salle d'armes" in Paris or London in those days from the old Italian schools of Queen Bess and Henri III, which men never left but covered with bruises, perchance minus an eye or a few teeth!' Perhaps we may see the final demise of the small sword, as the instrument *par excellence* for dealing

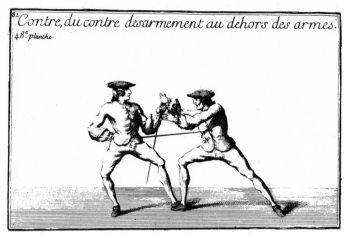

Contre, du contre desarmement au dehors des armes.
48.e planche.

Desarmement sur les coups de quarte au dedans des armes. 78.
45.e planche.

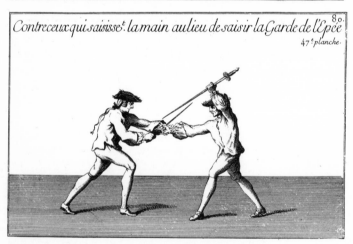

Contre ceux qui saisissent la main au lieu de saisir la Garde de l'Epée. 80.
47.e planche.

Methods of disarming in the French small sword fight.

out death in personal combat, in the dissolution of the *Compagnie des Maîtres en fait d'Armes des Académies du Roi en la Ville et Faubourg de Paris* – the French authority on matters of arms – during the Revolution, and the guillotining of its last syndic, Augustin Rousseau, in 1793. The Company had been in existence since the days of Charles IX. It had seen the decline of rapier play and the ascendancy of the small sword. It had seen the domination of Europe by French theory and practice. Now it was no more.

The *espada* – no more than a lighter version of the earlier rapier – still dominated Spanish play during the eighteenth century. It still retained its cutting edge, its cup guard and its *quillons*. The principles laid down by Carança and Narvaez some hundred and fifty years earlier still persisted.

Angelo, describing the Spanish fight of the late eighteenth century, says:

'The Spaniards have in fencing a different method to all other nations; they are fond oftern to give a cut on the head, and immediately after deliver a thrust between the eyes and the throat. Their guard is almost straight, their longe [lunge] very small; when they come in distance they bend the right knee and straighten the left, and carry the body forward; when they retire they bend the left knee and straighten the right; they throw the body back well, in a straight line with that of the antagonist, and parry with the left hand, or slip the right foot behind the left.

'Their swords are near five feet long from hilt to point, and cut with both edges; the shell is very large, and behind it is crossed with a small bar, which comes out about two inches on each side; they make use of this to wrench the sword out of the adversary's hand, by binding or crossing his blade with it, especially when they fight against a long sword; but it would be very difficult for them to execute this against a short sword. Their ordinary guard is with their wrist in tierce, and the point in a line with the face. They make

1   The small sword opposed to the pike.

2   The small sword and cloak opposed to the flail.

appels or attacks on the foot, and also half thrusts to the face, keep their bodies back, and form a circle with the point of their swords to the left, and straightening their arm, they advance their body to give the blow on the head, and recover instantly to their guard, quite straight, with their point in a direct line to their adversary's face.'

In many ways the *espada* bears a closer resemblance to the nineteenth- and twentieth-century duelling weapon than does the small sword, as can be seen in the illustration of the Marquis de Cuevas-Serge Lifar fight which took place in 1958. Since in Spain, as throughout Europe, the thrusting sword became almost exclusively the weapon of 'gentlemen', other weapons were used by lesser men. Castle ascribes the growth of Spanish fighting with the *navaja* – the long knife – to this fact.

In Italy, during the eighteenth and early nineteenth centuries, the position was similar. The small sword was the dominant weapon, and the French were supreme in their handling of it. Italian play continued to rely on much of the style of the earlier rapier play. The fighting style was vigorous and strong, relying on beats and binds on the opponent's blade and on a certain amount of opportunism.

Angelo – an Italian by birth – gives his view of Italian play towards the end of the eighteenth century:

'The Italian guard is commonly very low; they bend equally both knees; carry the body between both legs; they keep the wrist and point of the sword low, and have a contracted arm; they keep the left hand at the breast, to parry with it, and straightway return the thrust.

'Though this guard is natural to them, yet they vary every moment, to perplex their adversaries, in keeping a high wrist and point to the line of the shoulder; in keeping a high wrist and a very low point; and making large gesticulations of the body, and turning round their antagonist, some-

times to the right and sometimes to the left, or by an immediate advance of the left foot to the right; and they thrust straight thrusts at random, or make passes and voltes [side-steps]. They have much dependence on their agility, and the parade of the left hand: for that reason, when two Italians fight together they oftern are both hit together, which is called a counter thrust: this happens seldom with two good swordsmen, because they know how to find the blade by a counter disengage, or by the circle, and because they have a quick return.'

In Germany, the development was similar. The *Schwerdt* – the two-handed sword – the *Düsack* and the broadsword were replaced by the *Feder* or *Rappier*. The play was orientated more to the Italian than the French school. Nevertheless, play with the older weapons did continue and eventually developed into the purely cutting play of the *Schläger* in the nineteenth and twentieth centuries.

Unlike other countries in Europe, the places that kept alive the use of the sword for personal combat purposes were the universities. Castle considered that 'the amount of bloodshed caused among the pugnacious youth of Germany by the preposterous habit of wearing the sword instead of the gown in academic centres was hardly less than that brought about by the incomprehensible duelling mania which raged in France from the days of Henri II to those of Louis XIV.'

These university fencing schools were dominated by *Marxbrüder* and *Federfechter* – the two principal associations of German Masters of Defence. The *Marxbrüder*, a contraction of the *Bürgerschaft von St. Marcus von Löwenberg*, with its headquarters in Frankfurt am Main, was the older of the two with letters patent granted to it by the Emperor Frederick at Nürnberg in 1480. The *Federfechter* came into being in the sixteenth century and derived its name from the *Feder*, the German version of the rapier. Kahn, writing in 1739 as the authority on the German fencing schools, mentions Kreussler as the principal

The armed brawl, as the illustration makes clear, obeyed none of the niceties of the formal duel. Success was the only criterion and success was very dependent upon surprise. Here the principal figure has been run through the chest before he could raise his pistol to defend himself. His supporters fire pistols whilst their attackers begin to move forward armed with musket, swords, pistols and a hand-held bayonet. Of particular interest is the pistol man in the foreground who holds his top hat over the candle flame in such a way as to prevent its glare affecting the aim of his fellow ruffians. Such a gesture indicates that the man is not without considerable experience in this type of combat. From the nineteenth-century print, *The Cato Street Conspirators*. 'On the memorable night of 23 February 1820, at the moment when Smithers the police officer was stabbed. NB The scene faithfully represented from the Description of Mr Ruthven, the View of the Interior correctly sketched on the spot by George Cruikshank.'

The old guard positions and the possible attacks
from them according to Danet.

Origine des Gardes et Estocades anciennes.

1

Fig. 1.   *Fig. 2.*

L. G. Taraval sculp.   *Vaxeillere del.*

1.re Position.   *Garde.*

Planche 1.

2

Pl. 37.

Prime ancienne.   *Tierce ancienne.*

master of the seventeenth century. The family reigned over the whole German university scene from the early seventeenth until the late eighteenth centuries, rather as the Angelo family reigned in England during the second half of the eighteenth century and the beginning of the nineteenth. They taught at Jena, Leipzig and Giessen. Kahn himself was master to the university fencing schools at Goettingen and Helmstedt. The products of these schools were regarded as amongst the most formidable fighters in Europe.

Angelo gives his view of German play during the mid-eighteenth century:

> 'In the position of the German guard, the wrist is commonly turned in tierce, the wrist and arm in a line with the shoulder, the point at the adversary's waist, the right hip extremely reversed from the line, the body forward, the right knee bent, and the left exceedingly straight. The Germans seek the sword always in prime or seconde, and often thrust in that position with a drawn-in arm. They keep their left hand to the breast, with an intent to parry with it, and the moment they draw their sword they endeavour to beat fiercely with the edge of their sword on their antagonist's blade, with an intent to disarm them if possible.'

If we are to believe Castle, then 'it would seem as if, from the middle of the eighteenth century, fencing was quite the study of paramount importance at the university. At Jena, Halle, Leipzig, Heidelberg, and, later on, Goettingen, Helmstedt, and Giessen, duels were so common and so dangerous – the usual play being what we would call spadroon or cut-and-thrust fencing – that the most peaceable student was never sure of his life for a single day!'

Certainly cut-and-thrust play with the spadroon was highly dangerous. It is a wonder it lasted so long. But towards the end of the eighteenth century it was replaced in most universities by the *Hiebcoment*, a purely cutting weapon similar to the English back-sword of the same period.

1 The draw and the guard with the small sword in the late eighteenth century, according to Danet.

2 Attack in prime and tierce having their origin in old rapier play.

3 The salute taught by Danet.

3

1.ᵉ Position   SALUT   *2.ᵉ Position*

1. Position
2. Quarte
3. Tierce

3.ᵉ Position   *4.ᵉ Position*

'The students of Jena, however, as well as those of Halle and Erlangen, insisted on retaining the privilege of being killed or seriously wounded, instead of merely scarified, in their duels, and refused to be parted from their old-fashioned rapier till about the third decade of this century (the nineteenth).'

This cutting play developed into *Schläger* fighting, a version of which still persists today. Castle gives a lively account of nineteenth-century *Schläger* fighting:

'The Schlaeger is a basket-hilted sword with a long, *pointless*, flat and rather flexible rapier blade which, when used for duelling purposes, is sharpened for a length of seven or eight inches from the point on the right edge, and for about two inches on the false. The hilt is much larger than is usual in close-guarded swords, in order to allow a very free action of the wrist. The grip is made very thin near the hilt and somewhat thick at the pummel end, and provided with a loop, generally of leather, wherein the forefinger can be inserted, so that the Schlaeger may be held in a very easy, and, at the same time, very secure manner – this being the great desideratum in the *flipping* play of which its practice solely consists. In some universities a pair of diminutive *quillons* provided with *pas d'ânes* are in favour, instead of the loop, for the purpose of securing a firm grip.

'The adversaries fall on guard within close measure, holding their Schlaegers in a position of very high *prime*, with the arm fully extended and the point on a level with the mouth.

'The face and head being the only objective of the attack, a very elaborate system of armouring and padding is resorted to in order to protect the wrist, arm, and shoulders, and, in short, all parts of the body liable to receive by accident cuts aimed at the face, whose defence does not form part of this curious system of fencing. The eyes are protected by iron 'goggles', the branches of which likewise afford some protection to the temples. In some cases even, especially in duels

The methods of attack with the late eighteenth-century small sword.

Pl. 4. *Quarte haute dans les Armes*
PRIME DES MODERNES

Pl. 5. *Prime Ancienne*

Pl. 6. *Tierce haute*
SECONDE DES MODERNES

Pl. 7. *Seconde ancienne*
TIERCE BASSE DES MODERNES

Quarte basse des modernes.
QUATRIEME DES ANCIENS.
Pl. 8.

Pl. 9. *Quinte ancienne et moderne.*

Quarte dessus les Armes
ou Prime dessus les Armes

Quarte coupée hors les Armes.
ou Prime coupée hors les Armes.

Flanconnade

Botte de Quarte, touchée l'épée a la main.

Doublement sur faux relevement.

Effacement entier.

The disengagement by 'cut-over'.

The simple parries and other defensive movements recommended by Danet.

between *freshmen* – 'Füchse' – the head is further protected by a cap.

'The play is very simple, but so unnatural that it requires much vigour, long practice, and the development of particular muscles of the fore-arm, for perfection. It consists of flipping cuts delivered from the wrist – not with the centre of percussion, but with the extreme part of the blade, which alone is sharpened – and directed to either side of the adversary's face, and to the top or even the back of his head. At each blow the point describes nearly the whole circumference of a circle. . . .

'Parries are performed by raising the hand as high and as much forward as possible, still keeping the point very low, to meet attacks in high lines, and by shifting the opposition, to meet cuts attempted, under the point or otherwise, in low lines. The chief difficulty in parrying being, not merely to meet the opposite sword in time, but so to meet it as to prevent its point *flipping over*. Very little feinting is resorted to, but cuts are rapidly exchanged, success depending on the *vigour and rapidity* with which they can be returned. . . .

'A duel under these conditions is as much a trial of endurance as of skill, for no wounds on either side, excepting such as may be deemed really dangerous, are allowed to put a stop to the fight.'

The end of the eighteenth century and the beginning of the nineteenth saw increasingly the return to favour of the cutting sword. The light, curved blade of the Hungarian sabre allowed for fast action and a slicing rather than a chopping stroke. The sword, in fact, moved increasingly out of civilian circles and back into military. John McArthur, for example, writing in 1781, is clearly anxious to bring back into the navy proficiency in the use of the sword. More than many people of the period, McArthur has his eye firmly on training for actual combat. He recommends caution and coolness in a real encounter, and a series of figure-of-eight movements of the point – 'round

The simple parries and other defensive movements
(continued).

parades' in upper and lower lines. And, because of the real possibility of being attacked in the dark, he suggests a good deal of blindfold practice to get the 'feel' of an opposing sword.

The Revolution in France, as much as anything, was responsible for the return to the military rather than the civilian weapons. Harry Angelo devised a system for using the light cavalry sabre introduced from Hungary, and his son Henry 'interested himself in naval hand weapons, devising codes of instruction for the cutlass and the boarding-pike'. Spadroon play resulted in the re-introduction of many of the features of seventeenth-century rapier play. But despite attempts by such eminent military gentlemen in England as Captain Hutton and Colonel Matthey to bring back real skill into the use of the sword for combat, the weapon itself was redundant. Attempts were made into the late nineteenth century to establish the superiority of the sword over the rifle and bayonet, but without success. The reason, of course, was obvious. The crude firearms that Hope had mentioned at the end of the seventeenth century had become highly sophisticated. They were now accurate, reliable and deadlier than any sword.

Curiously, perhaps, the dagger did not follow the sword into limbo. It had been carried as a universal side-arm from the beginning of recorded history, useful not only in combat and hunting, but also at table. And it still had its uses. In the history of the dagger and its use in combat, we can see many of the principles governing the development and use of the sword. For example, we can again make the division into daggers using the point alone and those relying on both point and cutting edge. The misericorde, for example, the ballock dagger, the stiletto of seventeenth-century Italy, are all thrusting weapons. This fact argues special conditions in a fight. It argues either domination of the opponent by other means before the dagger is employed, or it argues a fight based entirely on an element of surprise. If, for example, an armoured man has been struck out of his saddle with his opponent's lance and lies

incapacitated on the ground, then his opponent can use his misericorde to kill him, or to demand surrender from him. But the misericorde is of little use until the armoured man is already incapacitated. In the use of the stiletto for assassination purposes, it is only effective as long as the victim is unaware that it is about to be used. It cannot be used defensively, as the sword can or as some other daggers can. Indeed, the only effective defence the stilletoist has, once his intention has been discovered, is flight.

By contrast with these purely thrusting daggers, is the much earlier *scramasax* of the Northmen, in vogue from the eighth to the twelfth centuries and for a good deal longer amongst the working people. It was an admirable multi-purpose weapon, being suitable for hunting and skinning animals as well as for fighting. Its long duration indicates how valuable it was felt to be. Generally it is a single-edged weapon with a broad blade at times reaching twenty inches in length. It could be used for both cutting and thrusting. No detailed records of the way in which it was used in combat appear to exist, though to judge from the weapon itself it could have been employed rather like the *Düsack* of sixteenth-century Germany, or the much later machete.

Writing of the use of the dagger and fighting knife in the Middle Ages, Peterson says:

'Little imagination seems to have been displayed in the manner in which the fighting knife was used. True, warriors did occasionally throw their daggers into the faces of the enemy before attacking with their swords, but in general the knife was a simple stabbing weapon. In a fight, one combatant usually tried to seize his opponent's knife arm with his left hand and hold it while he delivered his own blow. Strength rather than skill normally prevailed. Although a few contemporary portrayals of the dagger in use show it held with the blade above the hand in the modern knife-fighting manner, the overwhelming evidence indicates that it was usually held with the blade below the hand (a position in which the

thumb could be placed on the pommel of the weapon). Such a grip limited the wielder to an efficient downward stroke and an awkward horizontal stroke. All the flexibility and manœuvrability prized by later generations of knife-fighters were denied the man who held his dagger in such a position. More than anything it emphasized strength rather than speed. The one advantage of the downward stabbing stroke was that it could be delivered with more power than any forehand thrust, and this may have been overridingly important in a day when an opponent might well have been wearing a shirt of mail or some form of padded armour.'*

The dagger in combination with the sword is a different weapon in combat. We have seen that in the rapier fight it was used as the principal weapon of defence, and that it also had attacking possibilities. Silver, admittedly, thought it 'an imperfect ward', preferring the buckler to it, but he has no doubt about its lethal possibilities. When two rapiers are in engagement, he says, 'it is impossible to uncrosse, or get out, or to avoid the stabbes of the Daggers. And this hath falne out manie times amongst valiant men at those weapons.' The stab with the dagger is lethal, 'wherein', he considers, 'there lieth no defence'. Speaking specifically of 'Woodknives, Daggers, and such like short weapons of imperfect lengthes,' he considers, 'the longest have the advantage, because the fight of these weapons consist within the halfe or quarter Sword, wherein by the swift motions of their handes, their eyes are deceived, and in those weapons, commonly for their handes lieth no defence.'

Castle says of eighteenth-century Spain:

'Among the commoner devotees of the art of fence superiority began to be sought in the management of the dagger, when the monopoly of the sword was assumed by their betters.

* *Fighting Knives of the Western World* by Harold L. Peterson. Herbert Jenkins, 1968.

1-4 **The circular or 'counter' parries with the late eighteenth-century small sword.**

5 & 6 **Ripostes with the small sword after successful parries with the left hand.**

5

6

1 **The small-swordsman facing two opponents.**

2 & 3 **The Spanish style of sword play in the later eighteenth century according to Angelo.**

'To this we may ascribe the origin of the art of wielding the *navaja* – the long Spanish knife – which, when practised with the capa, was based on the principles of ancient sword-and-cloak play, and when alone, on those of the single rapier according to Carranza's teaching. In the first instance, the left arm, protected by two turns of the cloak, was used for parrying, the left foot when on guard being kept forward – the dagger was held in the right hand, thumb flat on the blade. In the second case, as there could be but little parrying except by seizing the wrist, true dexterity consisted in tempting the adversary into making some movement which might afford an opportunity for a time hit. On every occasion the stab was delivered by a pass.

'Much decision was required for this play, and perhaps even more real love of fighting than in the mathematical and philosophical rapier fence. Seville was reputed a great resort of proficients in the art of the dagger fight.'

In America a large, general-purpose knife was developing, useful for hunting, scalping, fighting and butchery. In many ways we may regard this knife and its use as the earliest American contribution to the history of personal combat. America had had no native theories concerning the use of the sword, although fights with that weapon certainly took place there, but in the field of knife-fighting – and later of pistol-fighting – she did make a significant contribution. Peterson

1

Garde Italienne.

88.

55.ᵉ*planche.*

1

Garde ordinaire des Espagnols.

90.

39.ᵉ*planche.*

2

4

1   The Italian guard according to Girard.

2   The typical Spanish guard.

3   The German guard with the small sword.

4 & 5   The Italian style of fighting with small sword and dagger according to Angelo.

3

5

A GERMAN STUDENTS' DUEL AT GÖTTINGEN

1

2

1 Duelling with the Schläger.

2 The fight with cutting swords.

3 The cutting sword opposed to the small sword.

4 The cutting sword opposed to the small sword and cloak.

99.*Ruse du pointeur, pour combatre l'Espadonneur en campagne.*
-5.ͤ *planche.*

3

4

The guard of 'carte', (1) the extension of the sword
arm and the lunge (2, 3) according to McArthur.
From *The Army and Navy Gentleman's Companion*.

I

2

3

The salute, the guard position and the fighting movements recommended by McArthur. From *The Gentleman's Companion.*

The inside Guard.

The positions of attack and defence in military broadsword play, advocated by Matthewson. It is interesting to compare the economy of movements and body positions here with those recommended by Fabris. As the theory and practice of swordplay progressed, variety of movements and guards was regarded as less and less of a virtue. From *Fencing Familiarised*.

1

Mr B — "seeking the Bubble reputation . — P. 5.

"the pulses' maddening play   And turn what some deem danger to delight
That thrills the wanderer of the trackless way   No dread of death, if with us die our foes
That for it self can woo the approaching fight   Save that it seems e'en duller than repose."   — Byron —

2

1 An affray with duelling épée, broadswords, dagger, buckler and hedge slasher.

2 Shipboard battle with pike, axe, cutlass, spadroon, small sword, pistol and musket. *Mr. B——— seeking the Bubble reputation* by Cruikshank.

3 The duel between Colonel Henry and Colonel Picquart in the late nineteenth century. Both men were involved in the Dreyfus case.

4 & 5 Duelling with the sabre and the épée in the late nineteenth century. From Hergsell's *Duell-Codex*.

3

4

5

1   Early seventeenth-century Italian stilettos. Victoria and Albert Museum.

2   English daggers of the sixteenth and seventeenth centuries. Victoria and Albert Museum.

3   Flemish, Italian and German daggers of the late fifteenth and early sixteenth centuries. Victoria and Albert Museum.

4   German dagger fighting of the sixteenth century. From Lebkommer's *Der Allten Fechter*.

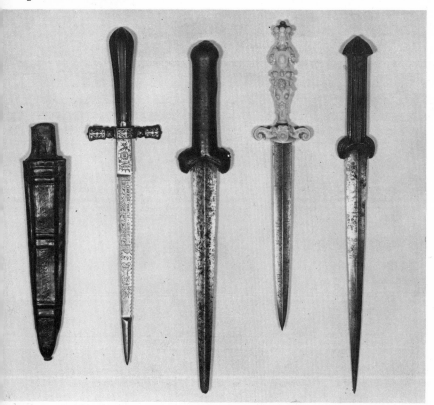

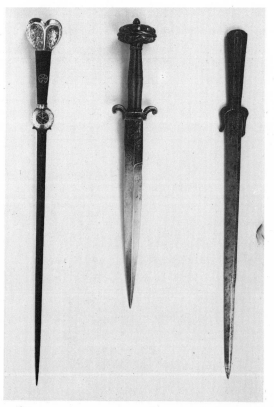

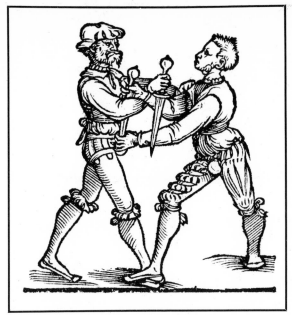

4

1 Dagger practice in the German school of fence in the sixteenth century. From Meyer's *Gründliche Beschreibung*.

2 The guard recommended by Marozzo for the dagger fight in the sixteenth century.

3 Italian dagger fighting in the early seventeenth century. A technique for disarming an opponent armed with a thrusting dagger. From Fabris' *Sienz E Pratica*.

4 An effective defence against an attack with the Bowie knife.

1

2

distinguishes two types of American knife during the later years of the eighteenth century. The first is double-edged, sharply pointed and equipped with *quillons*. The second, and perhaps the more important in view of the development of the Bowie knife in the nineteenth century, had the form of the modern French chef's knife. It was single-edged, sharply pointed and without any significant protection for the hand.

Peterson traces the birth of the Bowie knife proper to 1827 and with it James Bowie seems to have brought knife-fighting to perfection. The knife was a heavy, general-purpose instrument, suitable 'to attack another human, split a bear's skull, lop off a sapling with a single blow or dig in hard ground'. It was a single-edged weapon, sharply pointed and equipped with short *quillons*. The average blade-length was perhaps twelve inches. Some specimens, clearly designed more with human combat in mind than anything else, had complete knuckle-bows for hand protection. The technique of fighting with the single knife that originated in America is still accepted practice. It was taught for Commando fighting in the Second World War, and is still regarded as an important part of the training of such special troops. The illustrations of John Styers and A. J. Prizzi demonstrating knife-fighting give a clear idea of what modern combat with the weapon looks like. It is perhaps significant to notice that not once does Styers use his left hand in defence.

Styers and Prizzi show that in competent hands knife-fighting is undoubtedly an art. But Baldick gives an account which perhaps more accurately shows us what the average nineteenth-century knife-fight was like *in fact*. Barbier-Dufai and Raoul were officers in the French army. They quarrelled and fought inconclusively. Finally Dufai suggested – incredibly – that they should be roped together with their right arms left free, and put in a coach. Each man was to be armed with a poignard. 'The doors of the coach shall be closed, and at a given signal the coach will set off and go twice round the Place du Carrousel.'

3

'At the end of the second
round the seconds jumped down and opened the
door of the coach. The silence of death was
within, mid a sea of blood. Raoul was dead, and
Dufai also seemed to be dead; but he recovered
from the frightful wounds he had received. Raoul
had driven his poignard four times through the
Colonel's chest, and had hacked the lower part of
his person with his teeth.'

4

1 Styers and Sgt. Prizzi take the 'On-guard' position to begin the fight

2 Styers feints at the knee, forcing enemy to block

3 Quickly disengaging, he draws blood from left arm

4 Enemy takes backhander at Styers' head. Styers parries

5 Recoiling to free blade, Styers sees foe's arm exposed

6 He makes a quick cut and wounds his enemy for the second time

7 Balanced again, Styers awaits the next move

8 It comes. A wild uppercut which Styers avoids

9 He ignores the opening and reverses positions

10 He feints downwards at his opponent's leading leg

11 His opponent's guard drops to parry the feint

12 Styers slashes him blindingly across the forehead

13 And ends the fight with a disarming cut to the wrist.

8

9

10

11

12

13

Combat with the Japanese long sword in the nineteenth century. The illustration shows a single-handed attack with the point being parried by the sword held in both hands. All the agility and fierceness of Samurai sword play is expressed by the artist together with that ritualistic, dance-like quality which distinguished the Samurai as a professional warrior from the European swordsman. A point of particular interest is the way in which the defender receives his opponent's blade on the flat of his own. It seems that even in the perilous situation in which he finds himself here, he is still so deeply concerned about preserving the sharpness of the cutting edge of his own weapon that he will not allow it to come in contact with his opponent's blade even at the risk of reducing the strength of his parry. *The fight between Ariō Maru and Kameō Maru*. From the colour print by Kuniyoshi, about 1845, in the possession of the Victoria and Albert Museum, London.

1 The moves recommended by H. C. Angelo for the fight with the rifle and bayonet.

2 The sabre opposed to the bayonet. From H. C. Angelo's *Bayonet Exercise*.

3 The attack with the rifle and bayonet, the parry and riposte with the spadroon. From Matthewson's *Fencing Familiarised*.

2

3

1 **Modern bayonet practice. The Royal Scots.**

2 **The lunge with the modern rifle and bayonet. The Highland Light Infantry.**

1

2

The dagger and the knife have always required very close physical contact between the combatants, because of the shortness of their blades. The knife-fight has always had the appearance of what we might regard as armed wrestling, with all the savagery of tripping, gouging, kicking and striking in the face with the pommel. Speed and great physical agility have always been essential. The only knife-fight actually witnessed by the author had the appearance of a modern limbo dance.

The most widely used dagger, of course, has been the bayonet. In its development it has gone through a wide range of shapes and sizes, its blade has been wide and double-edged, short and single-edged, triangular and circular in section. Its method of attachment to the musket or rifle has varied from simply plugging its handle into the barrel, to the modern well-machined device for attaching it immediately below the muzzle so that the rifle can still be used for its principal purpose. Soldiers, by the way they have used it, have turned it into the kind of multi-purpose tool that earlier knives and daggers were. More recently, it has probably been used far more frequently for opening corned beef cans and cans of Coca Cola than for its original purpose.

But there has never been any doubt about the formidable nature of the bayonet when secured to the rifle and placed in practised hands. Hutton, who was certainly a very practised exponent of bayonet-fighting, is of the opinion that in a fight of bayonet against either broadsword or small sword, 'given equal skill and muscular strength to both combatants, the bayonet as a weapon must have the advantage, owing to its superior reach and greater momentum'. The rifle and bayonet is a much more manageable weapon than it may appear to a man inexperienced in its use. It is well balanced and can move with considerable speed. Because of its momentum, a strong parry is required to deflect it from its target once it has been committed. It is effective in defence; in attack, not only can it be used as a heavy thrusting weapon but strokes with the butt can be equally debilitating. In many ways its use is similar to that of the short pike and halberd.

Owen's poem, *Strange Meeting*, however, gives the tragic, terrible side of real combat with the bayonet:

'I am the enemy you killed, my friend.
I knew you in this dark; for so you frowned
Yesterday through me as you jabbed and killed.
I parried; but my hands were loath and cold.
Let us sleep now. . . .'

Chapter Nine

GUN FIGHTERS

The firearm, used in personal combat, can be regarded as a long-range thrusting weapon. By comparison with the sword its history is short and its development rapid. It took almost the whole of human history for the flint axe to evolve into the Hungarian sabre. Yet it took only a hundred and fifty years for the crude and inefficient pistol, whose use on horseback Hope had described, to evolve into the navy model Colt.

No complex theories of attack and defence with the pistol, comparable to those that we have seen with sword, could develop, for in essence the pistol is a much simpler weapon. As Silver said of the dagger, there is no defence against it. The command of a second in a pistol duel, 'Attend! Present! Fire!', sums up the whole activity. If the pistol was properly cared for, properly loaded and primed, it would fire. And if it fired, then the ball would either hit the opponent or it would not. If it hit him, he would be killed or seriously wounded, but if it did not then he would be completely unharmed. In the case of sword-play, when an attack has been launched on a vulnerable part of the target, the defender can still do something about it. He can parry, he can give a counter-thrust or he can dodge the attack. But when a pistol ball has been fired accurately, there is no defence against it.

True, there are many theories on how the target area may be reduced and how the effect of a hit may be minimised. Bosquett, for example, recommended a sideways stance so that the whole of the left side was protected by the right. The belly was to be drawn in, and 'at the same time the right hip twisted a little to cover and guard the lower extremities of the belly'. Even though such a stance did reduce the size of the target, it had its own disadvantages. Atkinson quotes the report from the *Freeman's Journal* of the pistol-fight that took place near Dublin on 2 February 1815, between Daniel O'Connell and J. N. d'Esterre:

'The friends of both parties retired and the combatants, having a pistol

1 The cartoonist's comment on the stupidity of many forms of duelling. The eighteenth-century small-swords man attempts to defend himself against the pistol man with the guard of his sword.

2 The duel with pistol and cloak as described by McBane. Both fighters hold the opposite ends of the cloak in their left hands and discharge their weapons at one another through it. If the pistols fired the outcome was certain death for both duellists. From *The Expert Swordsman's Companion*.

3 Rowlandson's view of the idiotic nature of duelling. Both duellists appear to be crouching in a grave in the certain knowledge that neither of them has a chance of leaving it.

1

2

3

in each hand, with directions to discharge them at their discretion, prepared to fire. They levelled and before the lapse of a second two shots were heard. Mr d'Esterre's was first and missed. Mr O'Connell's followed instantaneously and took effect in the thigh of his antagonist about an inch below the hip. Mr d'Esterre, of course, fell and both the surgeons hastened to him. They found that the ball had traversed the hip, but could not locate it. There was an immense effusion of blood. All parties prepared to move towards home and we need not describe the emotions which burst forth all along the road when it was ascertained that Mr O'Connell was safe. Mr d'Esterre's wound proved mortal – the ball passed through both thighs and there was violent hemorrhage of the bladder.'

If d'Esterre had not been standing in the approved way, reducing the size of his target by a sideways stance, the ball would at least not have gone through *both* hips.

The target size could also be reduced by a stooping posture, a concaving of the body so that the target height was reduced by five or six inches. But there was a limit to the way in which a man might cram his body into the smallest possible space, and beyond that limit other defensive factors had to be noted. The position, for example, of the pistol arm was important. If it was held a little bent and in the line of direct fire, then a ball which might otherwise lodge in the chest would first strike the arm. Even the position of the pistol and the hand were important; held in line with the target, they could offer some protection to the whole of the lower part of the face. But none of this was really 'defence', as we understand that word in connection with the sword, it was no more than taking every precaution to minimise the opponent's chances of success. It was an extension of the idea that one did not wear jewels to a duel, nor have one's buttons polished, nor have silver inlays on one's pistol, because all these would have provided one's opponent with a more precisely defined target at which to aim. They

were all precautions: they did not actually constitute defence, for against the bullet there is no defence.

Sir Jonah Barrington, writing in 1827 of an early pistol duel in which he fought, shows the dangers of not taking at least some of these elementary precautions. He gives some insight, too, into the activities of the second, the technique of aiming and the poor penetration of the ball:

'On arriving we saw my antagonist and his second – Jack Patterson, nephew of the Chief Justice, already on the ground. Daly wore a pea-green coat, a large tucker with a diamond brooch stuck in it, a three-cocked hat with a gold button loop and tassels, and silk stockings. A *couteau de chasse* dangled gracefully from his thigh.

'My second, Crosby, without any sort of salutation or prologue, immediately cried out "Ground, gentlemen! Damn measurements!" and placing me on his selected spot whispered into my ear: "Never aim at the head or heels. Hip the macaroni! The hip for ever my boy!"

'Daly took his ground about nine paces from me. He presented his pistol instantly, but gave me most gallantly a full front. I let fly without a second's delay. Daly staggered back two or three steps, put his hand to his breast and cried: "I'm hit, Sir!" He did not fire. We opened his waistcoat and a black spot, the size of a crown piece with a little blood, appeared directly over his breast bone. The ball had not penetrated, but his brooch had been broken and a piece of the setting was sticking fast in the bone. Daly put his cambric handkerchief, doubled, to his breast and bowed. I returned the salute and we parted without conversation or ceremony.'

It is questionable, of course, whether this form of fatuous activity comes within our concept of personal combat, any more than does 'Russian roulette' or the 'American duel' in which 'when two Americans wish to fight a duel, they load one

1 A nineteenth-century cartoon illustrating the natural advantages and disadvantages with which some duellists were endowed.

2 The tragic result of duelling. Hamilton makes the point that duelling had far wider effects than the mere defence of 'honour'. From *The Code of Honour*.

1

2

pistol, draw lots for it, and the winner shoots himself'. Consider, for example, Barrington's account of how he came to fight Daly:

'I received an invitation from Mr Daly to fight him early the ensuing morning. I had never spoken a word to him in my life and no possible cause of quarrel that I could guess existed between us. However, it being a decided opinion that a first overture of that nature could never be declined I accepted the invitation without inquiry.'

This, surely, was some form of dangerous game prompted by an odd sense of personal bravura. It falls into the same category as the child's game of 'dares' – 'I'll dare you to jump off this wall; I'll dare you to swim across that river'. It appeals to some gambling instinct – man pitted against danger, man pitted against death – and to judge from the number of duels fought by some men, and the frivolity of their causes, this peculiar form of gambling became no less compulsive than any other.

The strict rules of conduct, too, suggest some form of game rather than serious personal combat. Baldick gives the 'twenty-six commandments' of the Irish *code duello* of 1777 in full, in what must be regarded as the definitive work on the duel. The rules are very much those that have always applied to the duel. The seriousness of different types of insult are classified: to tell a man he is impertinent, for example, is less serious than to tell him he is a liar. More serious than an accusation of lying, is an actual physical blow. In the case of a duel arising out of an accusation of impertinence, only one shot from each party is required before the necessary apology can be made. By contrast,

'As a blow is strictly prohibited under any circumstances among gentlemen, no verbal apology can be received for such an insult. The alternatives, therefore, are: The offender handing a cane to the injured party to

3 A female pistol duel in the late eighteenth century. The hand and body positions adopted by the duellists are those of the small sword rather than the pistol. Compare the stances here with those in the Clemenceau-Déroulède duel.

4 The strange mixture of honour and bravado that motivated many duellists. The meeting between Pitt, Prime Minister of England, and Tierney, MP for Southwark, on Putney Heath in 1798.

1 The wounding of Sir Philip Francis by Warren Hastings, Governor-General of India, in a late eighteenth-century pistol duel.

2 The formal European duel of the early nineteenth century, with seconds and doctor in attendance and carriage waiting to transport the dead or injured party. From *The Life of a Nobleman*, engraved by G. Dawe.

3 The German military duel of the nineteenth century.

4 The duel between Clemenceau and Déroulède in the late nineteenth century, that arose out of the Dreyfus affair. Both men have adopted the classic stance of the European duellist. The sideways position of the body reduces the size of the target and the bent arm and high hand position shield the heart, throat and lower part of the face.

1

3

2

4

be used on his back, at the same time begging pardon; firing until one or both are disabled; or exchanging three shots and then begging pardon without the proffer of the cane. *N.B. If swords are used, the parties engage until one is well blooded, disabled, or disarmed, or until after receiving a wound and blood being drawn, the aggressor begs pardon.'*

The XIIIth commandment of this code is particularly interesting:

'Seconds to be of equal rank in society with the principals they attend, inasmuch as a second may either choose or chance to become a principal and equality is indispensable.'

It reminds us that in Europe duelling was an upper-class affair in which great importance was attached to equality of rank between the two duellists. The 'lower classes' did not duel. When they fought, they did so out of quite different motivation. It argues a common sense on the part of these lower classes that their social betters were denied.

The actual conduct of the duel was designed to provide the maximum possibility of a 'miss' without detracting from the pleasurable sense of danger. Seconds were 'bound to attempt a reconciliation before the meeting takes place, or after sufficient firing or hits as specified'. The signal to fire could be visual, in which case accurate aiming of the pistol was impossible, since the eye cannot be squinting along the barrel and watching for the drop of a handkerchief at one and the same time. Alternatively, it might be given verbally: 'Attend! Present! Fire!' The pistol was aimed on the 'Present!' but the time interval between that word and the command 'Fire!' was so short that again no proper aiming was possible. Thirdly, the duellists could fire 'at pleasure'. Some aim here was possible, but the longer one took to take accurate aim the more chance there was of one's opponent firing successfully first. Pistols were smooth-bored since the rifled barrel was much more accurate. They were loaded with a single ball, since multiple shot was more likely to hit the target. Even as late as 1858 John Wilson, in his *Code of Honor*, advocated the use of flintlock pistols because the chance of their inflicting a serious or fatal wound was less than with the percussion pistol. 'Percussion pistols', he says, 'may be mutually used if agreed on, but to object on that account is lawful.'

Wilson also gives a clear idea of the complexities of procedure in the pistol duel of the mid-nineteenth century, which turn the activity more into a game of bravado than into serious combat:

'Each second informs the other when he is about to load, and invites his presence, but the seconds rarely attend on such invitation as gentlemen may be safely trusted in this matter.

'The second, in presenting the pistol to his friend, should never put it in his pistol hand, but should place it in the other, which grasps it midway along the barrel, with the muzzle pointing in the contrary way to that which he is to fire, informing him that his pistol is loaded and ready for use. Before the word is given, the principal grasps the butt firmly in his pistol hand, and brings it muzzle downward to the fighting position.

'The fighting position is with the muzzle down and the barrel from you; for although it may be agreed that you may hold your pistol with the muzzle up, it may be objected to, as you can fire sooner from that position, and consequently have a decided advantage, which might not be claimed, and should not be granted.'

Wilson was writing of the American scene, and yet in America the business of personal combat with firearms seems to have been a good deal more serious – and in many ways a good deal more honest – than it was in Europe. The complex European conventions that turned killing and maiming into an elaborate game hardly existed in

1

2

3

4

America. Baldick quotes de Tocqueville as saying in 1831:

'In Europe one hardly ever fights a duel except in order to be able to say that one has done so; the offence is generally a sort of moral stain which one wants to wash away, and which most often is washed away at little expense. In America one only fights to kill; one fights because one sees no hope of getting one's adversary condemned to death. There are very few duels, but they always end fatally.'

The determination behind much American pistol duelling is apparent in the fight between De Witt Clinton and John Swartwout, which took place in New York in 1802. There were five exchanges of fire, during which Swartwout was hit twice in the left leg yet still refused to end the contest. Clinton at that point, however, refused to continue. It is perhaps of interest to note that both Swartwout's wounds were in the left leg, the leg that, according

1   **The German duel across marked parallel lines. From Hergsell's *Duell-Codex*.**

2   **The German duel from opposite sides of a single marked line.**

3–5   **The stages of the nineteenth century pistol duel in Germany.**

5

to the classic stance of European duelling, should have been entirely protected by the right. The duel between Alexander Hamilton, close friend of George Washington, and Aaron Burr, Vice-President of the United States, which took place in 1804, arose out of doubts cast by Hamilton on Burr's political integrity. Hamilton was killed by Burr's first shot and Burr, as a result of the killing, was disfranchised and charged with murder.

The difference between the European duel and that in America can be seen in the fight between Charles Dickinson and General Andrew Jackson. Dickinson fired first and Jackson was hit in the chest, though not seriously. Jackson took aim and his pistol misfired. He checked the misfire, took deliberate aim again and fired. Dickinson dropped dead. The European view of Jackson's action in continuing to fire after he himself had been hit, and after a misfire, was that 'having received Dickinson's bullet without any serious injury, it was not a just and fair thing in Jackson afterwards

to take deliberate aim at Dickinson and kill him'. However, the commentator concedes that 'the only excuse or justification I can find for General Jackson for his deliberate and premeditated killing of Dickinson is the fact that, perhaps, upon general principles, Dickinson ought to have been killed for slandering so upright and honourable a woman as the wife of General Jackson.' Both men must have known that the fight would end in the death of one or both of them. The intention behind it was wholly serious. They were not using those pistols that Hope had described a hundred years earlier. Indeed, on his way to the fight Dickinson had given a display of his brilliance with the pistol: 'at a distance of twenty-four feet, he fired four bullets into a space no bigger than a silver dollar'.

The seriousness of American fighting by comparison with many European encounters is apparent in the engagement between Maddox and Wells in Missouri in 1827. They fired two shots at one another, without doing any damage. It appeared that the quarrel had been settled, when the friends of the two men began to advance on one another. James Bowie – of knife fame – who was supporting Wells, fired at Colonel Crane, who was one of Maddox's friends. Bowie appears to have been hit in the hip. Crane then resting his pistol on his arm – hang the canons of formal duelling! – fired at General Currey, another of Wells' friends, and killed him. Bowie, drawing his famous knife, came at Crane whose pistols were now both unloaded, but was clubbed to the ground with the butt of one of them. Major Wright came in to support his friend Crane. He was carrying a sword-cane. He drew and thrust the sword at Bowie's chest. It struck the breastbone, but failed to penetrate. Bowie dragged Wright to the floor and stabbed him to death with his knife. A general fight between the supporters of the two sides ensued. In it six men – including General Currey and Major Wright – died, and fifteen were wounded.

This seriousness of intention in American personal combat extended far beyond the days of the

1 American revolver fighting. The idea of shooting a man before he presented his pistol would have been unthinkable to the formal pistol duellist in Europe.

2 The informality of the American pistol fight by comparison with the European.

3 A reconstruction of a Western gunfight. The positions of the gunfighters are of particular interest. None of the men adopts the stance characteristic of the formal European pistol duel. From the film *High Noon*.

flintlock and the percussion cap – a seriousness understandable in the context of the rapid development of the American nation westwards. As was inevitable, the law and accepted standards of behaviour lagged behind the actual physical progress. The ability to settle differences personally and on the spot was essential. An article published in the London *Lilliput* of February 1955 gives a very clear idea of how personal combat with the revolver differed from the formal European pistol duel. The writers conducted an experiment with a man who had taught secret service agents and saboteurs to kill with the pistol. This man was chosen 'because he seemed to approximate most closely to the bar-room killer of the Frontier. We decided that the best target shot in the country could not give us any line on the sheriff or gambler who did his killing indoors, in hot blood, without conventional aiming, against time, in cramped positions, and probably when badly scared.' Against two live targets, and using an unloaded gun, 'he pulled the trigger twice on each – both guinea pigs reported that the muzzle pointed exactly at their solar plexus – in a total of two and a half seconds'.

'His technique was this. The gun was held in the centre of the body at groin level. The elbow of the gun-arm was tucked into the right hip, the rest of the arm and hand being clear of the body. The fingers of the gun-hand gripped the butt until they were white; the wrist, in the demonstrator's words, was 'locked'. The gun, therefore, was as solid as if mounted in a gun turret. The only movement permitted to it was vertically up and down, like a railway signal. The locking of the wrist made it impossible for the revolver to be raised above the firing position.

'The firer's stance was exactly as shown in most Hollywood gunfights. He stood on the balls of his feet, weight a little forward, left hand extended slightly, palm open to help maintain balance. The whole impression was one of confident aggression, which attitude, he declared, was vital to success.

'He began our test with gun drawn, muzzle depressed towards the floor. On being ordered to engage both targets, he swung round until his shoulders were pointing squarely at his first enemy and only then brought the pistol up to the horizontal. He pulled the trigger twice. He then switched to the second man, swinging his body through 45 degrees. During this swing the gun was again depressed, only jerking up to fire when the shoulders were once more squarely on target. He again fired two shots, both of which would have killed.'

The principle of 'knowing one's pistol' has always been acknowledged by pistol-fighters from the earliest days of that weapon. Professional pistol-fighters 'worked on' the shape of the butt and on trigger pressure, to produce a weapon that exactly suited their individual needs. All of them stressed the need for daily practice. Wyatt Earp in his autobiography talks of 'practising for hours and hours', an activity which gave him a feeling of technical superiority in an actual fight and that essential coolness that allowed him to take a fraction of a second longer than his opponent to take exact aim, and hit with his first shot.

What this 'fraction of a second' amounted to in terms of actual time, can be seen from a demonstration that Ed McGivern, the American specialist, once gave. He drew a single-action Army Colt from its holster, aimed it, and fired a shot into a man-sized target at ten yards, in a quarter of a second. 'For a five-shot group covered by a man's hand after drawing at the same range – one and three-fifths seconds; for the same, but "fanning" the hammer – one and one-fifth seconds.'

This 'fanning' action was a technique favoured by some gun-fighters because of this fractional increase in the rate of fire that it gave. It consisted in keeping the trigger depressed – or in dispensing with the trigger altogether – brushing the hammer back with the heel of the hand and allowing the spring to carry it forward again into the firing position. If the movement was repeated rapidly it resulted in a rate of fire, as McGivern demonstrated, similar to that of some automatic weapons.

Pistol fighting on horseback. A conjectural American scene of the nineteenth century.

The disadvantage of 'fanning' was that the action might detract from the accuracy of the fire.

It is to America again that we must look for early examples of the use of the light machine-gun in personal combat. In the gang wars of Chicago, during American prohibition, it formed the backbone of many 'torpedoes', together with that other close-range phenomenon of the period, the sawn-off shotgun. It was a portable weapon, air-cooled, ideal for close combat. Machine-gun Jack McGurn, 'Capone's chief bodyguard and torpedo', earned his nickname from it. Allsop describes the use of both weapons in the St Valentine's Day Massacre in 1929:

'If not exactly full of dead men, the premises were littered with six and one dying man. They were among tyres and tarpaulins, at the foot of a wall hung with saws, files and electric flex. Five of the corpses were those of Pete Gusenberg, John May, Al Weinshank, James Clark and Adam Heyer, all Moran mobsters; their diamond tiepins and rings were undisturbed, their bankrolls had not been removed, their guns were in their holsters. The sixth body, still dapper with a carnation in its button-hole, was that of Dr Reinhart H. Schwim-mer, a young oculist, a crony and admirer of Moran, who lived at the Parkway Hotel on Lincoln Park West and who, like other citizens of the period, hung around with the gangs and enjoyed the raffishly romantic reputation that this gained him among his respectable friends. Three of the bodies, one with a hat in place, were in a neat line, sharing the cold concrete floor as if it was a warm bed; a fourth was crosswise at their feet; a fifth was huddled across a chair; the sixth was a few feet away, as if spun round by a heavy swipe from something, the seat of his trousers rather obscenely ripped open by a bullet.

'Indeed the swipe had been considerable. Post mortem examination showed that they had been sliced back and forth by more than a hundred machine-gun bullets; the line of fire, it was reported, had not deviated and had been "accurately sprayed between the ears and thighs; all were wounded in the head and vital organs". So thoroughly had the task been carried out that heads, bodies and limbs were almost severed by the slow and methodical stitching movement of the gun. To ensure the adequacy of the job, a shot-gun had also been employed. Clark and May had received a charge of buckshot apiece in the head. These were the sounds – the backfiring followed by the two thuds – that had been overheard by the neighbours.'*

In many ways, such an account is outside our definition of personal combat. Personal combat suggests an initial equality between the two parties, and in this case the dead men still had their own guns in their holsters. Yet in many ways it does illustrate the two important features in the use of firearms in combat: the importance of the element of surprise and the lack of defence against the bullet once it has been accurately fired. In some ways it demonstrates that all combat with firearms is outside our concept of personal combat, since in a sense success is not dependent on personal skill in the way that it is with the sword.

* *The Bootleggers* by Kenneth Allsop. Hutchinson, 1968.

A reconstruction of the St. Valentine's Day Massacre,
in which the two principal weapons of the actual
Massacre—the submachine gun and sawn-off shot-
gun—are illustrated. From the 20th Century-Fox film
The St Valentine's Day Massacre.

Chapter Ten

OTHER WAYS TO KILL A MAN

Personal combat, in our concept of it, has always required a certain equality between the combatants. It has always placed importance on the skill of the individuals concerned. A man skilled in the use of the sword or the halberd was more likely to defeat an opponent than one who was unskilled. Aerial combat comes within this definition. Combat between two fighter pilots is personal combat, and the skill with which they handle their aircraft and guns is a crucial factor in their survival.

When the first four squadrons of the Royal Flying Corps were sent to France in 1914 their function was seen as a purely reconnaissance one. They were 'scouts'. Their function was to collect information, about the disposition of enemy ground forces, that could not be obtained in any other way. Naturally, the denial of such information to them was important to the enemy. Their activities over the front line were resisted. Aerial combat was thrust upon them. The fighting equipment of their crews at that time was no more than that of the ordinary infantry officer – rifle and revolver. J. E. Johnson describes the kind of encounters that took place between British and German airmen during the first few weeks of the First World War, in a way that is oddly reminiscent of Sir William Hope's account of early pistol-fighting on horseback some two hundred years earlier:

'Having sighted his opponent, the pilot had to manoeuvre his machine into a position usually alongside the German, where the observer would have an opportunity to aim his rifle, and the firing range was sometimes only a few yards. The observer would force the upper part of his body into a slipstream of sixty or seventy miles an hour to swing and aim his rifle. Meanwhile the pilot produced his pistol and, with one hand on the stick, fired a few rounds for good measure.'[*]

The technique seems to have been more

Sixteenth-century unarmed combat according to Lebkommer. From *Der Allten Fechter*.

[*] *Full Circle* by J. E. Johnson. Chatto and Windus, 1968.

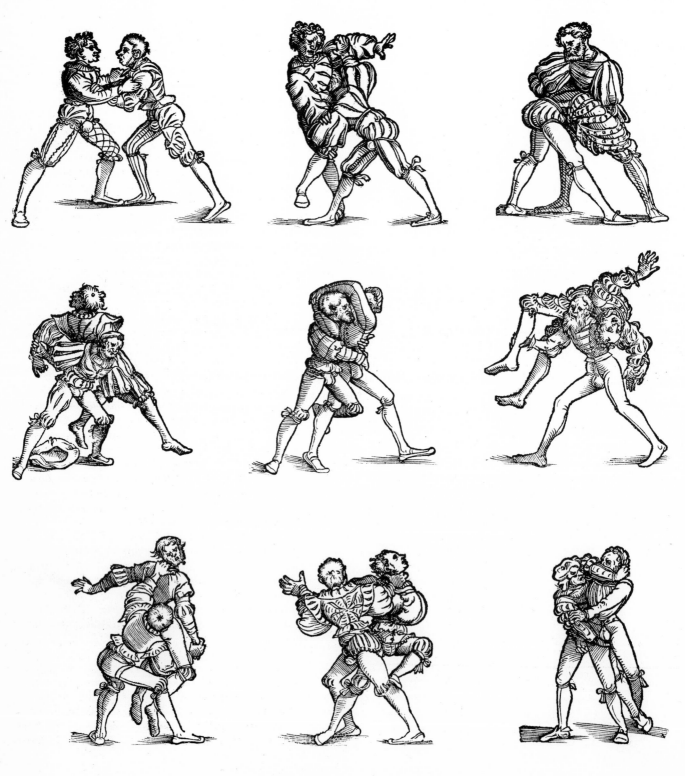

successful than Hope's pistol-fighting, since five enemy aircraft were destroyed by it during the first few weeks of the war. Yet it rapidly became apparent that some more efficient armament was necessary, and the R.F.C. began to equip its aircraft with the air-cooled Lewis machine-gun. This was official recognition of the fact that a new area of combat had been discovered and was about to be developed. Since it was new, the new principles embodied in it had to be learnt. Yet these principles did not become clear at once. On 6 July 1915 Oswald Boelcke and his gunner, Lieutenant von Wühlisch – who is reputed to have worn a red hussar's uniform under his flying kit – attacked a French two-seater inside the German lines. Boelcke had to manœuvre his Albatross so that Wühlisch could bring his gun to bear on it. He could not fly directly at the enemy, since this would have meant that Wühlisch would have been shooting off his own propeller. He had to manœuvre his plane rather like an old fighting ship, so that his gunner could deliver a broadside. Gun and aircraft were two separate things.

Anthony Fokker's E1 monoplane changed this concept. The aircraft was fitted with Fokker's new interrupter device which allowed a fixed machine-gun to fire through the propeller arc without hitting the blades. The line of fire coincided with the line of flight. The gun had no longer to be aimed independent of the movement of the aircraft. It was sufficient to aim the aircraft at the enemy and fire. Gun and aircraft became one. The aircraft itself was the weapon. From this new concept all the principles of fighter combat in the air evolved. In the first place, there were the natural features of the sky to be taken into consideration – sun and cloud cover. It very soon became apparent that a fighter attacking 'out of the sun', was almost impossible to see. In consequence, before committing himself to his first attack, a fighter pilot would try to position himself between his target and the sun. Such a position also gave him a height advantage, and height is speed, since an aircraft is at its

fastest in a dive. This superiority of speed allowed him to close with his enemy rapidly, so reducing the possibility of being seen, and after the attack to climb once more into a position of dominance. In the case of an attack on a single-seat aircraft, the aim was to drop into a position immediately behind it, open fire at something under two hundred yards, and break off the attack when it had fallen out of control, when its pilot had taken sufficient evasive action to carry it out of the attacker's sights, or when the distance between the two aircraft had become dangerously close. This position, following exactly the enemy's path through the sky, made him in effect a stationary target.

In the case of an attack on an aircraft with an observer and a rear-firing gun, the aim was to attack from behind but slightly below its line of flight. In this position the observer could not bring his gun to bear on the attacker, because of the danger of shooting off his own tailplane.

Defence, in the classic air combat of single-engined fighter versus single-engined fighter, was by avoidance. After the early battles of the Second World War, light armour-plating gave some protection from small-arms fire, but avoidance remained – and still remains – the principal defence. Provided a defending pilot sees an attacker slipping into the final firing position immediately astern, and before the attacker has actually fired, he can still take avoiding action. Such action has almost invariably taken the form of the steep and very tight turn. Such a manoeuvre carries the defender clear of the attacker's guns – at least for the moment – but it also gives him a chance of reversing the two positions. If he can turn more tightly than the attacker – turn 'inside' him – then he will eventually find himself behind his opponent: he will himself have become the attacker. The turn, of course, might be accompanied by a climb or a dive, depending on the capabilities of the two aircraft and the individual preference of the pilot.

In many ways the fighter pilot has much in common with the gun-fighter of the West. There

The destruction of a FW 190 by Flight Sergeant
Derek Erasmus of RAF Fighter Command, flying a
Second World War *Typhoon*.

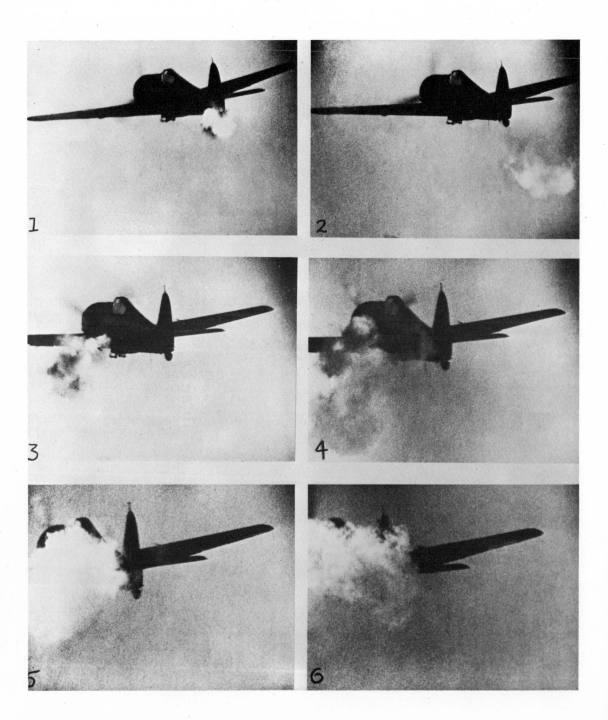

has always been a quality of individualism about him and about his fighting. Max Immelmann, for example, developed the 'Immelmann turn' as a technique of attack in which he could keep continuous height and speed superiority over an enemy. Boelcke developed a style of patient stalking in which he put himself in the ideal up-sun position before committing himself to the attack. 'Then his tactics were fashioned on the stoop of a hawk: he fastened on his victim from a long slanting dive, closing to short range and firing accurate, short bursts.' Albert Ball, in common with many fighter pilots since, spent a good deal of time working on his aircraft in order to drag a few more miles an hour out of it, and making sure that his gun was in first-class condition. His preparations for combat are reminiscent of the Western gun-fighter working on his gun to make it a fraction faster, a fraction more reliable, than that of his enemy. Baron Manfred von Richthofen 'based his tactics on good flying and accurate firing from short ranges'. In common with other fighter 'aces', there was a ruthless singleness of purpose behind him, and an obsession with his 'score' of enemy aircraft shot down.

Air Vice-Marshal J. E. Johnson, whose thirty-eight victories in air combat over Europe during the Second World War make him perhaps the best outstanding authority on the subject, attempts a classification of the outstanding fighter 'aces' from the start of the First World War to the end of the war in Korea. Richthofen he regards as 'the greatest air fighter of the First War', with Mick Mannock, James McCudden and the Frenchman René Fonck only a step behind. On the American side he lists Eddie Rickenbacker. Of the 'offensive air fighters of the Second War', Johnson considers Don Blakeslee of the United States Air Force to have been the greatest. On the German side, says Johnson, Adolf Galland was undoubtedly their 'greatest air fighter', together with such men as 'Pips' Priller and Werner Mölders. Of the R.A.F.'s 'aces', Johnson lists 'Sailor' Malan, the South African, as that force's 'greatest fighter pilot',

A Japanese *Zero* in a Kamikaze attack on a warship of the American Pacific Fleet during the Second World War.

1 & 2 The arms of the Samurai.

3 The arming of a Samurai. From a nineteenth-
century French print.

2

3

VENUS VICTRIX

together with Douglas Bader, and names as the two greatest night-fighter pilots John Cunningham and Bob Braham. Johnson himself must, of course, be added to such a list since, with thirty-eight victories, he was the 'Allied top scorer in Europe'.

We must remember, of course, that Johnson is concerned in his assessment with other factors than simply a man's skill in a dog-fight. He attaches great importance to 'leadership', to tactical ability and to the ability to teach others. For this reason Albert Ball, Billy Bishop and Georges Guynemer do not appear at the top of his list. 'These men fought emotionally from the heart, with impetuosity, never weighing the odds against them, and depended on superlative skill and marksmanship to shoot down their enemies. . . . Because they fought individually they never developed the qualities of leadership in the air.' We are not here concerned with the wider problems of warfare, but with personal combat. From our viewpoint, 'individuality' is not the disadvantage it is to Johnson, but rather the very essence of personal combat. From our more restricted viewpoint, then, such men might appear a good deal higher up the list of fighter 'aces'.

The activity of the Japanese *Kamikaze* is outside our terms of reference, though the motivation behind him is not. For a pilot to aim himself and his bomb-laden aircraft at the deck of a battleship and deliberately crash into it is not really personal combat, unless we stretch that concept to breaking-point. To the Western mind, such suicide, for whatever high motives, is more than can be asked of any man. Yet such a sacrifice is in the direct tradition of the *Kamikaze*'s predecessor, the *Samurai*.

Naturally, perhaps, we try to see the Samurai in European terms. We see him as the Japanese version of the European knight of chivalry, and certainly they have something in common. Both had a high place in society. Both were motivated by a strict code of behaviour. But there the similarity ends. There is something of the amateur about the European knight, a

sense that he dressed himself in armour and fought in the lists or at the Crusades only when he had nothing else to do. But the Samurai was a professional. He belonged to a military class whose sole activity was battle, a class that was well established by the twelfth century and only ceased to exist in its old form in the nineteenth. Even the codes of behaviour are different. The European knight was preoccupied with outward display – plumes, pennants, highly decorated armour and the whole visual magnificence that heraldry opened up. The Samurai, by contrast, was indifferent to all such show, to decoration, worldly goods and money. The Japanese soldier of the Second World War appeared slovenly and unkempt to European eyes. This was not, as many Europeans thought, because of a certain laziness and indiscipline in him. It was because, in the best Samurai tradition, he considered attention to dress unimportant if not actually effeminate. What the Samurai did think important was the development of masculine and serious qualities. His attitude to women, for example, was quite different from that romantic one of European chivalry.

Perhaps the Samurai had more in common with the old Viking *berserk* than with the gilded knight of chivalry. Both were great individualists. Both were entirely fearless. Both were devoted to the use of the sword and treated the weapon itself with a certain reverence. Both used personal battle-cries to bolster their own confidence and destroy that of the enemy. Yet here again the comparison ends, for the Samurai was puritanical and the Viking anything but abstemious.

Where the Samurai differed most from the European was in his attitude to suicide. Suicide to a European has always suggested a certain weakness, a certain shirking of responsibility. It is still frequently regarded in Europe as 'the easy way out'. To the Samurai, suicide was not only an entirely reasonable act, but at times the only possible one. And far from being 'the easy way out', self-disembowelment must have been one of the most painful of deaths, however sustained one might have been by indoctrination with a stoical philosophy from birth.

The Samurai fought with the bow, but the long sword was the classic weapon. It is a measure of the study that he gave to both the construction of the long sword and its use – travelling all over the country in search of a master who could advance his knowledge one more step – that perfection in both seems to have been reached by the eighth century. In the hands of the sword-smith Yasutsuna, says B. W. Robinson, 'the Japanese sword-blade became firmly established in the form it has retained ever since'. Of the weapon itself Robinson says:

'The Japanese sword-blade is proverbial for strength and sharpness, and whilst in many countries the sword has been highly regarded and richly adorned, the spiritual and symbolic qualities with which the Japanese blade has always been invested in the country of its origin, as well as its beauty of form and its terrible effectiveness, make it unique among the weapons of mankind'.

The Samurai carried two swords in combat, the long one for fighting and a shorter one for be-heading his vanquished opponent. The fight itself had something in common with early broadsword play. It was extremely active, as the illustrations of artists like Kuniyoshi and Japanese films like *Rashomon* show. But it relied far more on skill than did much broadsword play. Brute force, which was a characteristic of early broadsword play, seems never to have been a feature of Japanese sword-fighting. Again, where the early broadsword play was almost exclusively cutting, the Samurai fight relied on both the cut and thrust. Attacks accompanied by forma-lised cries were delivered with either one or two hands and 'the only effective protection against the two-handed stroke of a Japanese sword', according to Robinson, was that armour composed of dozens of overlapping metal and hide strips, that the Samurai wore in battle.

Defence against such attacks was by a parry with the sword, a counter-thrust or cut, or perhaps more usually by 'avoidance' – sidestepping and dodging. Such combat existed well into the nineteenth century, and not until 1877 was the wearing of the sword in public forbidden by Imperial edict.

The Samurai is particularly interesting in that he sheds a new light on the concept of the fighting man. The 'disarm' in European sword-play of the sixteenth, seventeenth and eighteenth centuries implies that a man who is deprived of his sword is no longer able to continue the contest. The Samurai rejected this view. He saw *himself* as a weapon, not necessarily needing some outside equipment to complete him. Without his sword he could still defend himself and disable his opponent with anything that came to hand. If necessary, he could use his own hands and feet, and his opponent's own efforts, as weapons. This highly developed skill is still the source out of which almost all modern unarmed combat springs. Certainly this view that the Samurai had of himself is one that is shared by the modern Commando and war-time 'agent'.

Less professional forms of unarmed combat have developed elsewhere, though the intention behind them has been only fractionally less serious than that of the Samurai and the Commando. Thomas Armstrong, in his novel *King Cotton* (Collins, 1962, p. 216) gives an alarming description of clog-fighting in northern England, and the psychological warfare leading up to it:

'While his hands were over his shoulders to strip off his shirt, Abel Nuttall joined in. "The fight's off if owt's barred," he said firmly.

'There was a guffaw from the ring-side. "You can take it for granted that everything's in," Chuck Smith jeered. "Pressing wi' the knees, tupping, strangling, all the bloody issue."

'"Clogs?" the engine-tenter persisted.

'That raised another hearty laugh. "Clogs, God aye," the youngest Bullock bellowed. "Yes,

1 The boxer of classical Greece. The gloves were designed to increase the power of the punch rather than cushion it as in modern boxing.

2 The first battle between Tom Paddock and Harry Paulson on 22 September 1851.

3 Fisticuffs in the early nineteenth century.

2

1 Bare knuckle men. A painting of Boughton and Figg by Hayall.

2 The opening round of the 39-round contest between J. L. Sullivan and Charlie Mitchell which took place in France in 1888. The result was a draw.

you'll damn' soon find out he isn't called the Clogger without cause. When he's poised your shin bones in. . . ."

'Abel was nodding with quiet satisfaction. "An' biting?" he next demanded. Reassured on that point, he had another question. "And gouging?" he said thinly, forcing a gleam of horrible anticipation into his deep-set eyes.

'"Gouging?" Jemmy Caffrey repeated uncertainly.

'"Aye, gouging." The engine-tenter smiled coldly.

'These preliminaries, coupled with the calmness of his opponent were not without effect on the other principal.

'"How's tha mean, gouging?" Clogger Lynch snapped.

'Abel Nuttall licked his lips anticipatorily.

'"Gouging," he began rather dreamily, "gouging is . . ." Finding an explanation too difficult in words, he gave a brief but nauseating demonstration, thumb and finger operating on his own eye. A quick twist of the wrist to show how it was done, subsequent to which he confidentially drew public attention to the outcome. "Plops out of t'socket as clean as a whistle. Easier than a ripe goose-gob coming away."

'"That's no English way of fighting," Clogger Lynch blurted out. . . .

'Without any warning his clog shot out, the iron-shod toe crashing into Abel Nuttall's leg immediately beneath the kneecap. From then, the full use of one limb denied him, the engine-tenter had the worst of it. An early blow split the side of his mouth, and another vicious swing caught him in the windpipe. It looked a safe bet that soon he would be unable to stand on his feet at all.'

No less fearsome was the practice of bare-knuckle fighting that took over when the gladiatorial combat with the sword fell into disrepute in the middle of the eighteenth century. The rules were rudimentary and the typical contest ended only when one of the fighters fell unconscious and could not be roused in the prescribed time. Haxlitt gives an account of the fight between Thomas Hickman and Bill Neate:

'They met again, and Neate seemed, not cowed, but particularly cautious. I saw his teeth clenched together and his brows knit close against the sun. He held out both his arms at full length straight before him, like two sledge-hammers, and raised his left an inch or two higher. Hickman could not get over this guard – they struck mutually and fell, but without advantage on either side. It was the same in the next round; but the balance of power was thus restored – the fate of the battle was suspended. No one could tell how it would end.

'This was the only moment in which opinion was divided; for, in the next, Hickman aiming a mortal blow at his adversary's neck, with his right hand, and failing from the length he had to reach, the other returned it with his left at full swing, planted a tremendous blow on his cheek-bone and eyebrow, and made a red ruin of that side of his face. Hickman went down, and there was another shout – a roar of triumph as the waves of fortune rolled tumultuously from side to side. This was a settler. Hickman got up, and "grinned horrible a ghastly smile", yet he was evidently dashed in his opinion of himself; it was the first time he had ever been so punished; all one side of his face was perfect scarlet, and his right eye was closed in dingy blackness, as he advanced to the fight, less confident, but still determined. After one or two more rounds, not receiving another such remembrancer, he rallied and went at it with his former impetuosity. But in vain. His strength had been weakened, – his blows could not tell at such a distance, – he was obliged to fling himself at his adversary, and could not strike from his feet; and almost as regularly as he flew at him with his right hand, Neate warded the blow, or drew back out of its reach, and felled him with the return of his left. There was little cautious sparring – no half-hits – no tapping and trifling, none of the *petit-maitreship* of the art – they were almost all knock-down blows: – the fight was a good stand-up fight.

'The wonder was the half-minute time. If there had been a minute or more allowed between each round, it would have been intelligible how they should by degrees recover strength and resolution; but to see two men smashed to the ground, smeared with gore, stunned, senseless, the breath beaten out of their bodies; and then, before you recover from the shock, to see them rise up with new strength and courage, stand steady to inflict or receive mortal offence, and rush upon each other "like two clouds over the Caspian" – this is the most astonishing thing of all: – this is the high and heroic state of man!

'From this time forward the event became more certain every round; and about the twelfth it seemed as if it must have been over. Hickman generally stood with his back to me; but in the scuffle, he had changed positions, and Neate just then made a tremendous lunge at him, and hit him full in the face. It was doubtful whether he would fall backwards or forwards; he hung suspended for a second or two, and then fell back, throwing his hands in the air, and with his face lifted up to the sky.

'I never saw anything more terrific than his aspect just before he fell. All traces of life, of natural expression, were gone from him. His face was like a human skull, a death's head, spouting blood. The eyes were filled with blood, the nose streamed with blood, the mouth gaped blood. He was not like an actual man, but like a preternatural, spectral appearance, or like one of the figures in Dante's *Inferno*. Yet he fought on after this for several rounds, still striking the first desperate blow, and Neate standing on the defensive, and using the same cautious guard to the last, as if he had still all his work to do; and it was not till Hickman was so stunned in the seventeenth or eighteenth round, that his senses forsook him, and he could not come to time, that the battle was declared over'.

The Samurai had established that, given sufficient determination, a man might turn anything into a weapon. Certainly as a species we have been highly inventive in the area of personal combat. The range of objects that we have produced for the sole purpose of attacking one another is almost limitless. The *chakhram* is an example of destructive ingenuity. In effect it is a metal quoit, a simple flat ring of steel, with the outer edge sharpened to form a continuous circular blade. It is a Sikh weapon and was carried on the turban. In use it was spun round the index finger and then launched at an opponent. The effect of the forward motion, together with the spin of the blade, was to produce a severe cut and at times actual amputation. The *tiger's claw* (*baghnak* or *wagh-nakh*) is similarly ingenious. Again an Indian weapon, it is in the tradition of the knuckle-duster though vastly more lethal. It consists of a metal bar some four inches long, to the flat of which are welded curved and sharpened 'claws'. Two rings are welded, one at either end of the bar, to take the index and little

fingers. R. F. Burton in his *Book of the Sword* (Chatto and Windus, 1884) describes the grip and use of one such weapon: 'Outside the hand you see nothing but two solid gold rings encircling the index and the minimus; these two are joined inside by a steel bar, which serves as a connecting base to three or four sharp claws, thin enough to fit between and to be hidden by the fingers of a half-closed hand. The attack is by ripping open the belly.' He quotes the following account of an actual nineteenth-century combat with tiger's claws between two Indian gladiators:

'The nude combatants were armed with "tiger's-claws" of horn; formerly, when these were of steel, the death of one of the athletes was unavoidable. The weapons, fitted into a kind of handle, were fastened by thongs to the closed right hand. The men, drunk with Bhang or Indian hemp, rushed upon each other and tore like tigers at face and body; forehead-skins would hang in shreds; necks and ribs would be laid open, and not unfrequently one or both would bleed to death.'

Men have fought one another with bull whips and in South America they have fought with the *bolas*, that ingenious weapon composed of two or three balls on the ends of rope. Men have fought in Ireland with the *shilelah*, a weapon with its own unique fighting style, the first object of which 'is generally to knock the hat off, in order to get at the head'. *Single-stick* play, or *back-swording*, was used in the nineteenth century in quite serious combat. Perhaps the best account in print of the principles of such play in the west of England is that in *Tom Brown's Schooldays*:

'The weapon is a good stout ash-stick, with a large basket handle, heavier and somewhat shorter than a common single-stick. The players are called "old gamesters" – why, I can't tell you – and their object is simply to break one another's heads; for the

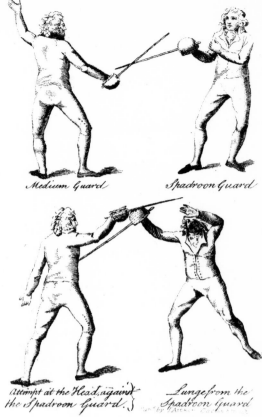

Hanging Gourd.   *St Georges Gaurd.*

Medium Guard   *Spadroon Guard*

Cut outside the Legf   *Second Position*

Attempt at the Head, against the Spadroon Guard.   *Lunge from the Spadroon Guard*

Single-stick play according to Matthewson. From *Fencing Familiarised*.

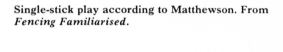

Lunge from the hanging Guard, the Parry with the left hand

Desarm from the Hanging Guard

moment that blood runs an inch anywhere above the eyebrow, the old gamester to whom it belongs is beaten, and has to stop. A very slight blow with the sticks will fetch blood, so that it is by no means a punishing pastime, if the men don't play on purpose, and savagely, at the body and arms of their adversaries. The old gamester going into action only takes off his hat and coat, and arms himself with a stick; he then loops the fingers of his left hand in a handkerchief or strap, which he fastens round his left leg, measuring the length, so that when he draws it tight with his left elbow in the air, that elbow shall just reach as high as his crown. Thus you see, so long as he chooses to keep his left elbow up, regardless of cuts, he has a perfect guard for the left side of his head. Then he advances his right hand above and in front of his head, holding his stick across so that its point projects an inch or two over his left elbow, and thus his whole head is completely guarded, and he faces his man armed in like manner, and they stand some three feet apart, often nearer, and feint, and strike, and return at one another's heads, until one cries "hold", or blood flows; in the first case, they are allowed a minute's time, and go on again; in the latter, another pair of gamesters are called on. If good men are playing, the quickness of the returns is marvellous; you hear the rattle like that a boy makes drawing his stick along palings, only heavier, and the closeness of the men in action to one another gives it a strange interest, and makes a spell at back-swording a very noble sight.'

Men have fought with razors, bicycle-chains – the modern equivalent of the flail – and coshes. Writing of the fight with the constable's truncheon, Hutton says:

'It is essential to consider on what parts a blow may be most advantageously planted in order to terminate the fight at once. A blow on the side of the head with a stout truncheon would very likely prove fatal, and I should not advise its use except in the case of very extreme necessity, and an upward cut at the point of the jaw would be nearly as conclusive.

'The best points to strike at, are those where bone is prominent, such as the collar-bone, the point of the shoulder, the elbow and forearm, the right hand, and, which might perhaps be overlooked, the advanced knee either inside or outside – but should this be attempted, great care must be taken to avoid a counter on the head; a thrust at close quarters in the pit of the stomach would be effective, and the pummel might be applied on the head or face.'

This is a substantial part of our history as human animals, the way in which we have pondered on how we might kill or seriously injure one another. We have done it in the name of Church, State, honour, chivalry and justice, but the real motive has usually been to preserve or increase our self-esteem. To succeed in personal combat, to vanquish an opponent, has always been accompanied by increased self-esteem, and despite the social restrictions that have increasingly been placed upon this form of behaviour, such success has always enhanced our position within our social group. Even failure in combat – provided the failure is 'honourable' – can carry a certain enhancement of self-esteem. The same is true of nations. Belgium was vanquished in 1914, yet because her failure to withstand the advance of a superior enemy was seen to be 'honourable', it raised her in the esteem of her neighbours and therefore in her own eyes. It is perhaps significant in this context to note that the massive monument on Thiepval ridge in northern France was erected to those who fell in the Battle of the Somme in 1916, not to those who lived through it to victory. The same is true of most of the war monuments of Europe.

The use of the word 'history' is perhaps misleading. It implies the study of a development that is finished. Something in the past. Yet personal combat is still very much with us, though its form has changed. There are still

Aerial combat of the First World War. It will be seen from the illustration that all the fighter aircraft are attacking from behind and that three of them are dropping from above in order to gain forward speed by diving. The classic method of meeting such attack is by means of the steep turn towards it. Alternatively a rear-firing machinegun position could be mounted as is shown here. The disadvantage of this method of defence is shown in the case of the fighter in the bottom left-hand corner of the picture who is able to engage the enemy whilst being out of the arc of fire of the defending machinegunner. From the painting *Cutting Out His Eyes* by G. Davis in the possession of the Imperial War Museum, London.

Aerial combat in the Second World War

1. Frontal or rear attack when perfectly timed could be highly effective. Fire was concentrated on the enemy plane's most vulnerable areas, such as crew cabins and engines. However, the combined closing speed of perhaps 600 m.p.h. allowed for only one second's firing time, begun at 400 yards range, before the attacking pilot was obliged to make his anti-collision manoeuvre.

2. Attack from an oblique angle demanded good shooting, with deflection aiming to allow for the enemy aircraft's speed in relation to the attacker's. Due consideration had always to be given to the positioning of the Germans' defensive armament and armour. Experienced fighter pilots were adept at aircraft recognition and they remembered a plane's strong and weak points.

3. Diving attack through an enemy formation called for snap aiming. Once again allowances had to be made for the rapidly moving targets. But as the attackers dived through the enemy formation they presented only a fleeting opportunity for retaliatory fire, while their build-up of speed allowed the fighters to pull up to a commanding height before returning to the attack.

4. Attack from the side called for full deflection aiming. Passing fast behind the enemy, who had probably just been raked with fire, the fighters again offered little opportunity to enemy marksmen to swing their fire. Once clear, the attackers could manoeuvre for a follow-up assault. Crews of German bombers were grouped in frontal areas and were highly vulnerable.

5. Attack out of the sun meant that the enemy gunners were either unaware of the impending approach of R.A.F. fighters or were dazzled to such an extent that they were unable to take proper aim. But often the tables could be turned when the enemy's escort fighters, lurking at an even greater altitude, could in turn dive from the sun and the hunters found themselves the hunted.

6. Dogfights were not always won by the fastest aircraft. Manoeuvrability counted for even more than sheer speed. The Spitfire, for instance, had a smaller turning circle than the faster Me 109 or the Me 110. Combats often developed into an ever tightening circle with each pilot trying to get on the tail of his opponent. In such tight turns the participants had to beware of sudden blackouts.

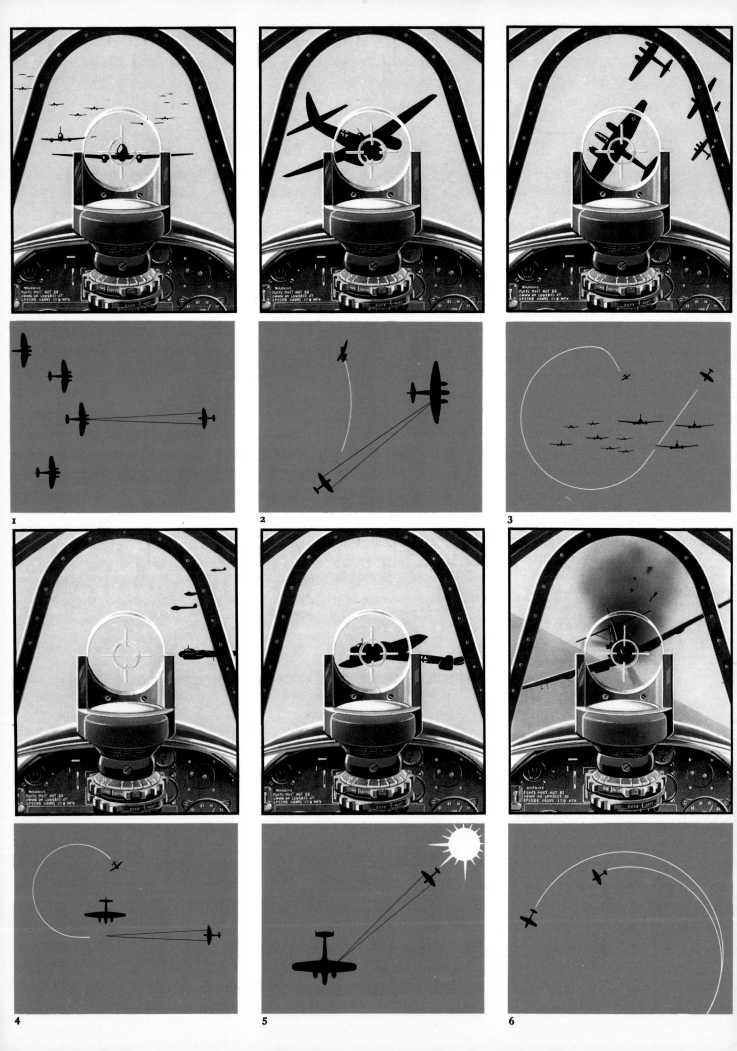

1

2

3

4

5

6

The thrust with the walking cane. From *Anti-pugilism.*

Antipugilism

occasions when combat takes on its old physical forms, of course. On 14 July 1969, for example, the *Daily Telegraph* reported a knife-fight that took place in Bradford in which one man died and another was wounded. On 4 September 1969 *The Times* reported that Senor Pedro Cersosimo, the Uruguayan Minister of the Interior, had been challenged to a duel by Senor Adolfo Aguirre Gonzalez, dean of the university school of architecture in Montevideo, on the grounds that the latter had suffered 'a personal insult and demanded reparation in "the field of honour"'. Senor Cersosimo very sensibly declined the challenge. But such occurrences are rare today. The weapon of the later years of the twentieth century is psychological. In itself this is not new. The Samurai, screaming his superior ancestry at his opponent, understood the principle of psychological combat. The Viking *berserk*, uttering his blood-curdling battle-cries, was employing the same weapon. Goliath bragged before doing battle, bayonet charges have been accompanied by pipe music and drum-rolls, the Western gunfighter affected a swaggering arrogance – all for the same purpose, to demolish at least some of the enemy's confidence. But all employed such psychological techniques as a prelude or an accompaniment to actual *physical* combat. The psychological weapon was not sufficient in itself to demolish an enemy.

If our century has dropped the sword and the pistol it has certainly refined the psychological weapon. The most cursory glance through press reports of divorce court proceedings is sufficient to show how widely it is used and how very effective it can be over a period of time. We read of cases where one human being has destroyed another in every human sense except the physical one, without the slightest bruising of the skin. And no one who has sat regularly on committees will be unaware of the intensity and fury of the psychological combats taking place in them, conflicts which can destroy a man quite as effectively as any sword ever did.

The age of Elizabeth I of England was a violent one. Yet if we care to look at it our own age is no less violent. George Silver, Joachim Meyer and Donald McBane were violent men, yet we have men of our own who could match them in violence. The difference lies in the forms that modern violence takes. It takes those forms because our attitude to ourselves has changed. We believe, it seems, that we have civilised ourselves beyond violence, beyond those animal aspects of our natures that still held our ancestors. Yet the facts of contemporary life do not support such a view. To this extent we are more hypocritical than the old sword and pistol men, or more misguided. God forbid that we should ever again see sword and buckler men going at one another in the streets, or hear the crack of pistol-fire from the woods, but from our ancestors who engaged in such activities we might still learn something. We might learn that however objectionable the fact might be, however much it might conflict with the view we have of ourselves, we are none the less violent animals, and any description of man that ignores his violent side is incomplete.

BIBLIOGRAPHY

AGRIPPA, CAMILLO, *Trattato di Scienza d'Arme*, Venice, 1604.

A HIGHLAND OFFICER, *Anti-Pugilism*, London, 1790.

ALFIERI, FRANCESCO FERO., *La Scherma*, Padova, 1640.

ALLANSON-WINN, R. G. and PHILLIPPS-WOLLEY, C., *Broadsword and Singlestick*, London, 1890.

ALLSOP, KENNETH, *The Bootleggers*, London, 1961.

ANGELO, DOMENICO, *L'Ecole Des Armes*, London, 1763.

ANGELO, HENRY, *Hungarian and Highland Broadsword*, London, 1798.

ANGELO, HENRY, *The Reminiscences of Henry Angelo*, London, 1830.

ANGELO, HENRY, *Angelo's Pic Nic*, London, 1834.

ANGELO, HENRY C., *Angelo's Bayonet Exercise*, London, 1857.

ATKINSON, JOHN A., *Duelling Pistols*, London, 1964.

AYLWARD, J. D., *The House of Angelo*, London, 1953.

AYLWARD, J. D., *The English Master of Arms*, London, 1956.

AYLWARD, J. D., *The Small-sword in England*, London, 1960.

BALDICK, ROBERT, *The Duel*, London, 1965.

BARRINGTON, SIR JONAH, *Personal Sketches of His Own Time*, Dublin, 1827.

BESNARD, CHARLES, *Le Maistre d'Arme Libéral*, Rennes, 1653.

B(LACKWELL), H., *The Gentleman's Tutor for the Small Sword: or, The Compleat English Fencing Master*, London, 1730.

BOSQUETT, ABRAHAM, *The Young Man of Honour's Vade-Mecum*, London, 1817.

BOWOOD, RICHARD, *Soldiers Soldiers*, London, 1965.

BURKE, EDMUND, *The History of Archery*, London, 1958.

BURTON, SIR RICHARD F., *The Book of the Sword*, London, 1884.

CAPO FERO, RIDOLFO, *Gran Simulacro dell' Arte è dell' Uso della Scherma*, Siena, 1610.

CARANÇA, HIERONIMO DE, *De la Philosophia de las Armas*, Lisbon, 1582.

CASTLE, EGERTON, *Schools and Masters of Fence*, London, 1885.

DANET, GUILLAUME, *L'Art des Armes*, Paris, 1767.

D'AVILLIER, CHARLES and DORÉ, GUSTAVE, *The Navaja and its use in Spain*, London, 1881.

DONOVAN, FRANK, *The Vikings*, London, 1964.

ETTENHARD, DON FRANCISCO ANTONIO DE, *Compendio de los Fundamentos de la Verdadera Destreza, y Filosofia de las Armas*, Madrid, 1675.

ETTENHARD, DON FRANCISCO ANTONIO DE, *Diestro Italiano, y Español, Explican sus Doctrinas con Evidencias Mathematicas, Conforme a los Preceptos de la Verdadera Destreza, y Filosofia de las Armas etc.*, Madrid, 1697.

FABRIS, SALVATOR, *Sienz e Practica d'Arme*, Copenhagen, 1606.

FFOULKES, CHARLES and HOPKINSON, CAPT. E. C., *Sword, Lance and Bayonet*, Cambridge, 1938.

GIGANTI, NICOLETTO, *Teatro*, Venice, 1606.

GILCHRIST, JAMES P., *A Brief Display of the Origin and History of Ordeals*, London, 1821.

GIORGETTI, G., *Armi Bianche*, Milan, 1961.

GIRARD, P. J. F., *Traité des Armes*, La Haye, 1740.

GODFREY, CAPT. JOHN, *A Treatise Upon the Useful Science of Defence*, London, 1747.

GRASSI, GIACOMO DI, *His True Arte of Defence*, London, 1594.

GROSE, FRANCIS, *Military Antiquities*, London, 1786.

HAMILTON, JOSEPH, *Some Short and Useful Reflections Upon Duelling by a Christian Patriot*, Dublin, 1823.

HAMILTON, JOSEPH, *The Code of Honour as Approved by Several Gentlemen of Rank, Courage, Experience and Discretion*, London, 1824.

HAMILTON, JOSEPH, *The Royal Code of Honor for the Regulation of Duelling*, Dublin, 1825.

HAMILTON, JOSEPH, *The Only Approved Guide Through All Stages of a Quarrel*, London, 1829.

HAYWARD, JOHN, *Swords and Daggers*, London, 1951.

HERGSELL, GUSTAV, *Die Fechtkunst*, Vienna, 1881.

HERGSELL, GUSTAV, *Unterricht im Säbelfechten*, Vienna, 1885.

HERGSELL, GUSTAV, *Duell-Codex*, Vienna, 1891.

HOLMES, M. R., *Arms and Armour in Tudor and Stuart London*, London, 1957.

HOPE, SIR WILLIAM, *The Compleat Fencing-Master*, London, 1710.

HUTTON, CAPT. ALFRED, *Cold Steel*, London, 1889.

HUTTON, CAPT. ALFRED, *The Swordsman*, London, 1891.

HUTTON, CAPT. ALFRED, *The Sword and the Centuries*, London, 1901.

JOHNSON, J. E., *Full Circle*, London, 1964.

KAHN, ANTHON FRIEDRICH, *Anfangsgrunde der Fechtkunst*, Goettingen, 1739.

LABAT, *L'Art de l'Epée*, Toulouse, 1690.

LACOMBE, PAUL, *Arms and Armour*, London, 1869.

LEBKOMMER, HANS, *Der Allten Fechter gründtliche Kunst*, Frankfurt am Main, 1529–36?

LIANCOUR, ANDRÉ WERNESSON DE, *Le Maistre d'Armes*, Paris, 1686.

LOCKHART, GEORGE, *The Lockhart Papers*, London, 1817.

MCARTHUR, JOHN, *The Army and Navy Gentleman's Companion*, London, 1780.

MCBANE, DONALD, *The Expert Sword-Man's Companion*, Glasgow, 1728.

MACLAGAN, ERIC, *The Bayeux Tapestry*, London, 1943.

MANCIOLINO, ANTONIO, *Opera Nova*, Bologna, 1531.

MARCELLI, ANTONIO, *Regole Della Scherma*, Rome, 1686.

MAROZZO, ACHILLE, *Opera Nova*, Venice, 1550.

Mars His Feild or The Exercise of Armes, London, undated.

MATTHEWSON, T., *Fencing Familiarised, or, A*

Treatise on the Scottish Broadsword, Salford, 1805.

MATTHEY, COL. CYRIL G. R. (ed.), *Works of George Silver*, London, 1898.

MAZO, BONDI DI, *La Spada Maestra*, Venice, 1696.

MEYER, JOACHIM, *Gründtliche Beschreibung der freyen Ritterlichen und Adelichen kunst des Fechtens in allerley gebzeuchlichen Wehren mit vil schönen und nützlichten Figuren gezieret und fürgestellet*, Strassburg, 1570.

MILLER, CAPTAIN J., *A Treatise on Fencing*, London, 1738.

NARVAEZ, D. LUYS PACHECO DE, *Libro de las Grandezas de la Espada*, Madrid, 1600.

OAKESHOTT, R. EWART, *The Archeology of Weapons*, London, 1960.

OAKESHOTT, R. EWART, *The Sword in the Age of Chivalry*, London, 1964.

OLIVIER, M., *Fencing Familiarized*, London, 1771.

On Fencing with the Two Handed Sword, MS. Harl. 3542.

PERCHE, JEAN BAPTISTE LE, *L'Exercise des Armes ou le Maniement du Fleuret*, Paris, 1676.

PETERSON, HAROLD L., *Daggers and Fighting Knives of the Western World*, London, 1968.

PISTOFILO, BONAVENTURA, *Oplomachia*, Siena, 1621.

PISTOFILO, BONAVENTURA, *Il Torneo*, Bologna, 1627.

RICKETTS, HOWARD, *Firearms*, London, 1962.

ROBINSON, B. W., *Arms and Armour of Old Japan*, London, 1951.

ROLAND, GEORGE, *Treatise on the Theory and Practice of the Art of Fencing*, Edinburgh, 1823.

ROWORTH, C., *The Art of Defence with Broadsword and Sabre*, London, 1798.

Rules and Regulations for the Sword Exercise of Cavalry, London, 1796.

SABINE, LORENZO, *Notes on Duels*, Boston, 1859.

SAINCT DIDIER, HENRY DE, *Traicte Contenant les Secrets du Premier Livre sur l'Espée Seule etc.*, Paris, 1573.

SAVIOLO, VINCENTIO, *His Practise*, London, 1595.

SEGAR, SIR WILLIAM, *The Book of Honor and Armes*, London, 1590.

SILVER, GEORGE, *Paradoxes of Defence*, London, 1599.

SINCLAIR, CAPTAIN, *Cudgel-playing Modernised and Improved*, London, 1800.

SJØVOLD, THORLEIF, *The Oseberg Find*, Oslo, 1957.

STONE, GEORGE CAMERON, *A Glossary of the Construction, Decoration and Use of Arms and Armor*, New York, 1961.

SUTOR, JAKOB, *Künstliches Fechtbuch*, Stuttgart, 1849. (Original edition Frankfurt am Main, 1612.)

SWETNAM, JOSEPH, *The Schoole of The Noble and Worthy Science of Defence*, London, 1617.

THIBAULT, GIRARD, *Academie de l'Espée*, Leyden, 1628.

THIMM, CAPT. CARL, *Bibliography of Fencing and Duelling*, London, 1896.

TOUCHE, PHILIBERT DE LA, *Les Vrays Principes de l'Espée Seule*, Paris, 1670.

UDEN, GRANT, *A Dictionary of Chivalry*, London, 1968.

VIGGIANI, ANGELO, *Lo Schermo*, Venice, 1575.

WALKER, DONALD, *Defensive Exercises*, London, 1840.

WEBSTER, GRAHAM, *The Roman Army*, Chester, 1956.

WILKINSON, FREDERICK, *Small Arms*, London, 1965.

WILKINSON, FREDERICK, *Swords and Daggers*, London, 1967

WILKINSON, HENRY, *Engines of War*, London, 1841.

WILSON, JOHN, *Code of Honor*, 1858.

WISE, ARTHUR, *Weapons in the Theatre*, London, 1968.

WYLDE, ZACHARY, *The English Master of Defence etc.*, York, 1711.

ACKNOWLEDGEMENTS

The author and publishers are indebted to the following sources for permission to reproduce the illustrations listed:

Bodleian Library, Oxford
29, 30, 36, 37, 38, 40, 41, 42, 43, 44, 46, 51, 52, 53, 54, 55, 58, 59, 60 (1), 103, 135 (2), 142 (1, 2 & 4), 143 (6 & 8), 162, 180, 182, 183, 198 (1 & 2), 199 (3), 201 (3), 212.

British Museum, London
16, 22, 32, 34, 50, 56, 57, 64, 67, 68, 70, 71, 72, 73, 75, 76, 77, 78, 79, 80, 81, 82, 83, 84, 85, 87, 88, 89, 90, 91, 92, 93, 94, 95, 96, 97, 98, 99, 100, 101, 102, 106, 108, 109, 110, 111, 112, 113, 114, 115, 116, 118, 120, 121, 122, 123, 124, 125, 134, 135, 136, 137, 138, 139, 140, 141, 142 (3 & 5), 143 (7 & 9), 163, 164, 165, 166, 168, 169, 170, 171, 173, 174, 175, 176, 178, 179, 197, 198 (4), 199 (5), 201 (4), 208 (2), 209 (4 & 5), 211, 213 (3), 226, 227, 232, 234.

Mary Evans Picture Library
12, 15, 23 (2), 61, 146, 200 (1), 213 (4), 224 (1 & 3), 229 (1 & 2), 230.

Imperial War Museum, London
236, 237.

National Film Archives, London
28, 229 (3).

National Library of Scotland, Edinburgh
47, 48, 49, 153, 154, 155, 185, 186, 187, 188, 189, 190, 191, 192, 194, 195, 196, 202, 203, 204, 205, 206, 207, 216, 217, 220 (2), 247, 249.

Phaidon Press Ltd
24 (1), 25 (1).

Radio Times Hulton Picture Library
23 (3), 24 (2), 25 (3 & 4), 27, 200 (2), 208 (1), 209 (3), 218, 220 (1 & 3), 222 (1), 223, 224 (2 & 4), 238, 239, 240, 243, 244.

Römisch-Germanisches Zentralmuseum, Mainz
18, 19.

Twentieth Century-Fox Film Company Ltd.
231.

University Library, Edinburgh
127, 128, 129, 130, 131, 132, 144, 147, 148, 149, 150, 151, 158, 159, 160, 161.

Victoria and Albert Museum, London
35, 60 (2), 62, 66, 104, 105, 133, 156, 157, 177, 210.

COLOUR PLATES

John R. Freeman
facing page 9 (bottom); between pages 56 & 57.

Mary Evans Picture Library
facing page 177 (bottom).

Mansell Collection
between pages 184 & 185.

Transworld Feature Syndicate Inc.
facing page 249.

INDEX